How To Build A Kick-Ass Advertising Agency

Peter Levitan

Portlandia Press
Portland, Oregon

How To Build A Kick-Ass Advertising Agency

Copyright © 2023 by Peter Levitan. All rights reserved.
Published in the United States of America.

No part of this book may be used or reproduced in any manner whatsoever without written permission except in the case of brief quotations embodied in critical articles and reviews.

ISBN: 978-0-9883119-8-5

Portlandia Press
Portland, Oregon

Table of Contents

Chapter 1 What the Hell Is Advertising?

1   What Are We?
5   Why Do We Do This?

Chapter 2 The Advertising Agency Business Plan

9   Start Here
11   Nine Elements of a One-Page Business Plan

Chapter 3 Agency Positioning Power

15   It's An Agency Positioning Jungle
16   Distinction vs. Sameness
16   The Expert Agency
17   eatbigfish: The Challenger Expert
18   Positioning Options
19   The Elevator Pitch

Chapter 4 Marketing Starts Here

21   Nail These Big Three

Chapter 5 Please Be Unignorable

27   Thank You, john st.
28   Getting to Unignorable

Chapter 6 Thought Leadership

31   Thinking Works
32   Thought Leadership Is Good
33   Thinking Is Tough Work
34   The Unignorable Insight
34   Building Insights
36   18 Insight Tools

Chapter 7 You Inc.

39   Only You Own You
40   Your Personal Brand and Business
40   Advertising's Personal Masters
44   What about You?
47   "The Brand Called You"
47   Six Branding Platforms

Chapter 8 Intellectual Property

57   Basecamp and Money
58   IP and Growth
60   Productizing the Agency

Chapter 9 24/7 Business Development

65   Stop with the Shoemaker Excuse
66   Building the Plan
68   A Deep-Dive Assessment

Chapter 10 The Optimal Agency Website

71	Always Revising
72	Generalizations First
72	The 10-Second Website Rule
73	Three Optimized Elements
78	Website Navigation
90	The Power of Landing Pages

Chapter 11 Inbound or Outbound Marketing?

91	Oh My. In Out. What to Do?
92	Inbound Marketing = Attraction
93	Outbound Marketing = Direct Marketing
94	Do Both? But...

Chapter 12 Account-Based Marketing

97	Four Mantras
98	ABM = Direct Marketing = Sales
99	The Art of Prospecting
101	Leverage Buyer Intent
102	ABM Timing and Cadence

Chapter 13 Inbound Marketing

107	It's All about Attraction
109	A Wide-Open Inbound Opportunity
110	Have A Public Relations Plan

Chapter 14 Marketing Insight Distribution

116	Deliver The Insights
121	My Distribution Bottom-Line

Chapter 15 Process Wins

123   Process Rules Business Development. Full Stop.
125   Your Agency Is Your Client
125   Two Management Tools

Chapter 16 Agency Talent Management

127   It's the People, Stupid
128   The Art of Retention
129   To Remote or Not to Remote?
134   Workplace Solutions
135   Three Easy People Management Tactics
137   Three Ridiculous Insanities
140   Manage Boss Burnout

Chapter 17 Recruitment

143   The Art of Recruitment
146   The Onboarding Dilemma
148   The Power of Culture
151   Diversity, Equity, and Inclusion

Chapter 18 Community Spirit

157   The Art of Philanthropy and Your Ad Agency

Chapter 19 Client Management

161   What Do Clients Want?
163   What Type of Agency Does the Client Need?
166   How Much Should a Client Spend?
170   What More Do Clients Really Need?

Chapter 20 The Savvy Account Manager

- 173 Why Clients Split
- 174 The Account Manager Role
- 176 Account Management Training

Chapter 21 Show Me the Money

- 181 Savvy Accounting
- 182 Your Agency: A Bottom-Line Model from AMI
- 183 Back To How to Price
- 187 Cost Management

Chapter 22 The Business Development Budget

- 189 A Sad Biz Dev Story
- 190 Budgeting for Business Development
- 191 Do Not Pitch That Account
- 193 Do a Client Assessment

Chapter 23 The Business Development Director

- 195 74% Failure Rate Blues
- 196 What Can We Do?

Chapter 24 How to Build, Buy, and Sell an Agency

- 199 Build Your New Agency
- 201 The Agency Name Game
- 206 Brand Name Development
- 208 Buy An Agency
- 208 Sell Your Agency

Chapter 25 Only One Interview

- 223 Going Into Orbit

Chapter 26 A Special Gift for You: Two Instructive Stories

227   The Worst Advertising Agency Presentation—Ever
235   A Sad Ad Man "Bye-Bye" Story

Chapter 27 Resources

239   Best Advertising Creative Brief
243   Agency Positioning Statements
246   The Go-No-Go Pitch Quiz
250   Sample Business Development Director Agreement

The Author

A Coda

Introduction

Peter to AI: "Does the marketing world need a new book about how to run a profitable and happy advertising agency?"

AI: "It's difficult to say whether the world really needs a new book on how to run an advertising agency. However, if the book offers unique insights, valuable advice, and practical tips, it will be an invaluable resource for people in the advertising industry or those interested in starting their own agency."

Peter to AI: "Who should write the comprehensive book on advertising agency management?"

AI: "The best candidate to write a book about how to run and grow an advertising agency would be someone who has a deep understanding of the advertising industry, someone who has run an agency and can provide practical, actionable advice to those looking to start or run their own successful agency. It would also help if that person was also an advertising agency client.

According to my assessment, that person is Peter Levitan."

Peter on Being Kick-Ass.

I settled on the title *How To Build A Kick-Ass Advertising Agency* because it gets to the point.

My *The Levitan Pitch. Buy This Book. Win More Pitches.* got to the point too and delivered actionable advice. So does this book. I have a bias towards action.

I use the term *kick-ass* to describe a person or company that is high-energy, impressive, people-first, smart, exciting, effective, perceived as an industry leader and profitable.

Being kick-ass is the most efficient path to success.

Peter on Timing.

Publishing a book sets its views and facts *in perpetuum*. *Kick-Ass* includes expert quotes, relevant third-party research, and industry statistics to support my thinking and advice. Although our industry's facts and figures shift daily, I believe my information is evergreen as it supports a discussion of the advertising industry's ongoing issues and opportunities.

Yes, the industry and what we do has shifted in the past few years. An understatement. That said, what we ultimately do for our clients hasn't. We help them grow their awareness, build their brands, and sell stuff.

CHAPTER 1

What the Hell Is Advertising?

What Are We?

Do you remember when simply saying that you are an advertising agency defined your business? You made ads and your mom understood what you did for a living.

After I decided to name this book *Kick-Ass*, I had to decide what to call the advertising industry itself. Today we all make much more than just ads. So, what will you tell Mom?

Here's a list of what today's advertising agencies call themselves—and things can get confusing, especially given service synergies:

- Advertising agency
- Ad Agency
- Full-service agency
- Integrated agency

CHAPTER 1

- Marketing agency
- Digital agency
- UX/UI agency
- Influencer agency
- Storytelling agency
- Media planning and buying agency
- Creative agency
- Branding agency
- Social media agency
- Web design agency
- SEM agency
- SEO agency
- PPC agency
- Email agency
- MarTech agency
- TikTok agency
- Direct marketing agency
- eCommerce agency
- Recruitment agency
- CRO agency
- B2B agency
- Challenger brand agency
- Promotion agency
- Out-of-home agency
- Design agency
- Experiential agency
- Strategic consultancy agency
- Performance marketing agency
- AR/VR agency
- Public relations agency
- Strategic consultancy
- AI agency
- In-house agency

WHAT THE HELL IS ADVERTISING?

Yikes. That's thirty-three options. To help me position and title this book, I turned to Google Trends to see what marketing agency identifying terms future client types might search for. I'll admit I was surprised to see that "marketing agency" was the clear search-term winner, followed by "digital agency," "advertising agency," and then "ad agency."

"Marketing agency." Really? With this information in hand I was hard pressed to find even a handful of agencies that called themselves a marketing agency.

Given the search results, why don't more agencies call themselves marketing agencies? Not sexy enough? Too broad?

What about the word agency itself? The descriptor agency seems a bit outdated, as it refers to the days when agencies acted as media buying agents. However, the descriptor agency remains in wide use:

BBH Global:
"We are a creative agency obsessed with making your brand more valuable."

adam&eveDDB:
"A creative agency dedicated to making work that works."

The Stable:
"The STABLE is an ecommerce agency that connects brands and consumers across all channels."

Billion Dollar Boy:
"Billion Dollar Boy is a global influencer marketing agency that specializes in integrated, creator-led advertising."

We Are Social:
"We are a global socially-led creative agency based out of New York City with unrivaled social media expertise."

CHAPTER 1

Elves:
"We are a B Corp certified, integrated creative agency for ambitious brands."

Some agencies do get past the word *agency*:

WPP:
"We are the creative transformation company."

Omnicom:
"Omnicom is a global leader in marketing communications."

Viral Nation:
"A modern marketing & technology company."

eatbigfish:
"eatbigfish is a global strategic brand consultancy specializing in challenger brands and business."

Koto:
"We are four creative studios across the globe."

What do industry search consultants call the types of marketing services companies they search for and advise clients to look at? The consultants avoid the need for clarification and complexity by just saying *agency*.

AAR:
"The industry's leading agency search consultants."

Roth Ryan Hayes:
"Roth Ryan Hayes is a leader in the field of agency search, selection, and compensation."

Select Resources:
"Premier consultancy in agency search and relationship management."

R3:
"We help marketers find, pay and keep the best possible agency relationships – covering Creative, Media, PR, Digital, Social, Performance, Event, Promotions and CRM."

Me? I like to keep things simple, as in using the tried-and-true descriptor *agency*, as in: *How To Build A Kick-Ass Advertising Agency.*

Why Do We Do This?

People go into the advertising business for many reasons. Here's my take on why we do this. I'll start with me (this is my book after all).

Before I got into advertising, I owned a professional photography studio in San Francisco with a client list that included Visa, Mondavi, and *San Francisco* magazine. Nice clients, but I was not having fun. I didn't want to shoot for money. Especially in a studio.

On a visit to my New York home, my parents' apartment building doorman and I talked about life (very NYC) and my goals. I mentioned that I thought of going into advertising. He said, "Wow, have I got a guy for you." He introduced me to my parents' neighbor Maxwell "Mac" Dane, a founder of today's DDB, née Doyle Dane Bernbach.
I met Mac at his huge Madison Avenue office, and he said, "Hey kid, yup, advertising is cool." Even with this positive message, he didn't offer me a job.

Around that time, my brother-in-law was a marketing director at Mars, Inc. He had me visit a super sharp three-piece-suited account guy at the huge Times Square Ted Bates agency. It was obvious *he* was having serious fun. He said, "Hey kid, go into advertising." That said, Ted Bates didn't offer me a job.

CHAPTER 1

OK, I'll spare you the rest of the story, which included some Levitan direct marketing aimed at agency decision makers. I eventually landed a position as an assistant account executive at Dancer Fitzgerald Sample, New York's largest agency, on the General Mills account. DFS was a *Mad Men* agency that even pitched against Don Draper in the *Mad Men* TV show.

I stayed at DFS, which morphed into Saatchi & Saatchi Advertising Worldwide. Sixteen years at one company.

Back to the why we do this advertising stuff. We all have our reasons. Here are mine:

1. Working in advertising just happens to be fun. Albert Einstein got it way right: "Creativity is intelligence having fun."
2. It's a fast-paced environment.
3. It's a creative problem-solving business with a diversity of assignments. New ideas and solutions are developed daily.
4. It combines art and science.
5. Advertising shapes culture. We are immersed in studying culture.
6. Advertising is a people business. It helps people, brands, and companies tell their stories and, importantly, grow. We get paid to do this.
7. It is both local *and* global.
8. It is on the forefront of technology.
9. There are many paths. You could work for an Omnicom agency or as a digital nomad in Chiang Mai.

Sometimes we move so fast (sometimes too fast) that we forget how much fun advertising can be. And should be.

Oh, The Money

Making huge bucks is generally not the reason people work in the advertising business. That said, the advertising world does generate a decent living. The US Bureau of Labor Statistics' latest data lists median pay at $133,380. A *decent* living, but not near the average compensation of a Google employee at $280,000. One more number. Good news, the median pay for lawyers is $127,990. That's $5,390 less than advertising.

Another reason people enter the adverting world is that the business of adverting has a low cost of entry. It doesn't require a bucket of capital to join, open, or buy into an agency.

A BFA graduate can just walk in the door at most agencies. Today, degrees might not even matter. A self-trained Atlanta-based WordPress specialist can open a website shop with a digital shingle in a couple of hours. Compare this to the lawyers I mentioned earlier. They spend on average $60,000 per year for three years of law school to land that entry-level position.

Do *you* need a college degree to make it in advertising? No. From the savvy people at ADWEAK:

> BREAKING: Parents Not Sure Why They Spent all That Money on College Education for Daughter to Be "Storyteller."

We Are Creative

Advertising people are creative. Full stop.

From the Oxford Dictionary (not from me because I am not creative enough to define the idea of creativity):

> The use of the imagination or original ideas, especially in the production of an artistic work.

I could argue with the narrow definition of using *artistic* work. But, what the hell. W+K's Old Spice work is artistic. Dollar Shave Club's "Our blades are F***ing Great" was artistic.

We become strategists, media planners, production directors, account managers, even CFOs because it is a creative endeavor. An endeavor that requires imagination and original ideas.

CHAPTER 1

And Let's Not Forget: Fun Is Good

I'll go back to my belief that a key reason we're in advertising is because it is a seriously fun way to make a living.

However, to make advertising truly fun we must remember that it is still a business. A well-run business. And that's why you need a business plan.

CHAPTER 2

The Advertising Agency Business Plan

Start Here

Now that you know the what and why of advertising, it's time to craft a business plan for your agency. Your plan will define your objectives and how you'll achieve your stated goals.

After dealing with mucho advertising, design, digital, and PR agencies over my career, I can safely tell you that most agencies do not have a master business plan. If they once had one, they do not have an updated version. Not having an updated plan that recognizes industry shifts and new opportunities is a bad idea that will most likely impede your revenue quest.

My own Portland agency didn't have a detailed plan. I had a good idea of what business we were in and what type of accounts we wanted, but we didn't have a written plan. I should have, even if just a one-pager that

CHAPTER 2

was reviewed and updated every year. Why update? Well, think about the evolution of the advertising marketplace. Or if you prefer today's vernacular—transformation.

"Advertising world transformation?" you ask.

1. The first TV commercial was run by Bulova Watch Company in 1941. It had 4,000 viewers in New York.
2. The first digital ad was a 1994 banner ad for AT&T on the Hotwired website. Get this: It had a click-through rate of 44%. The ad asked, "Have you ever clicked your mouse right here? You will." We did.
3. The first mobile ad was an SMS text shared by that Finnish company in 2000.
4. Google launched AdWords in 2000. Just a bit of transformation.
5. What did the industry look like in December 2019? Generally optimistic.
6. Only three months later the industry feared Covid would be the norm.
7. How we communicate with each other has experienced a major shift. Zoom alone has over 350 million daily meeting participants.
8. In October 2021 Facebook went Meta.
9. In 2022 TikTok users averaged 95 minutes per day (over 1.5 hours) on the platform, and 1.85 minutes per session.
10. 2023? Think AI: DALL·E 2, Jasper, Stable Diffusion, ChatGPT, anyone? More arriving every day. Need an AI agency to help out here? Switzerland's AvantGrade calls itself an "AI first" digital marketing agency.
11. 2024 and beyond? Scenario planning, anyone?

Why didn't my agency have an evolving master business plan? I didn't think I had the time. Clients came first. Lame on my part. But don't feel bad for me. We did make a good living.

Do *you* have a business plan? Having a strategic plan will help you define your mission, market, services, sales proposition, financial goals, and agency structure. The plan will help you manage your time and staff and inform your recruitment and talent management system.

Sounds like a lot of work. But it doesn't have to be. In fact, keeping the plan simple is a path worth following.

Nine Elements of a One-Page Business Plan

You do not need a tome-like business plan. Tome? I like this definition of *tome:* "a book, especially a very heavy, large, or learned book."

No heavy binders please. Follow the advice of Winston Churchill.

Winston was known for his insistence on having his ministers write one-page memorandums to get to the point. As he said to his war cabinet, "It is slothful not to compress your thoughts."

If Churchill could run a war effort from one-pagers, you can get your plan on one sheet of paper. In this case the adage "Keep it simple, stupid!" applies.

Getting to KISS. Just respond to these prompts with one or two sentences.

1. **What is your mission?**
   What is your agency's service offer?
   An example from Goodby Silverstein & Partners: "Our mission is to create experiences that reach millions and even billions but seem to speak only to you. We call this effect mass intimacy."

2. **What is your vision?**
   What are your core values?
   Again, from GS&P, "We are a creative company that puts people at the center of everything we do. We work with both clients and consumers in an atmosphere of honesty and truth, wiping away preconceptions and learning together."

CHAPTER 2

3. **Brand positioning**
   Define your brand. Your specific expertise. Your competitive advantage. Distill down to a brief elevator pitch that provides distinction and a strong competitive message. Your agency personality.

   Strive to be unignorable. Strive to get past sameness.

4. **Your services**
   What services do you provide that will help clients meet their objectives? How can you create service differentiation? What marketing benefits do you deliver?

5. **Marketing**
   What is the desired outcome or your business development program? How will you become famous and desired (and rich)? Can you create a secret sauce?

   Define your ideal prospect and customer profile. Be focused. Be realistic. Strategies, marketing channels, and technology will be detailed in your master business development plan.

6. **Financial projections**
   Define your profit margin goals. Plus 20% would be nice. Build out those pricing strategies. Manage cash flow, agency costs, cash reserves. Build a P&L and balance sheet.

7. **Staff requirements**
   Will you need full-time employees, contractors?
   Build staff utilization projections. How will you recruit? How will you train your people?

8. **Office requirements**

   Will you have a full or part-time office? How will you reduce uncertainty? How will you manage and inspire remote workers?

9. **Define success**

   What are your success metrics? Types of clients? Awareness? Profitability? Build to sell? Fun tracking? Have a goal line.

Review and Adjust

Your business plan should deliver a clear path to success. And most of the details should be *kinda* set in stone. However, shit happens, and you'll need to keep abreast of evolving market forces that might cause you to have to make midstream adjustments. Market forces? To name a few...

- Recessions. I've lived through a few.
- Evolving office and staff scenarios.
- Media shifts à la see ya Facebook, hello Meta. Next? Will Congress eventually kill TikTok? If gone, who replaces its massive activity? YouTube Shorts? Instagram Reels?
- Data privacy legislation and its impact on advertising.
- The repeal of Section 230.
- Digital disruption? AI copywriters, AI art directors, and virtual reality.

Some market-rocking forces will be impossible to predict: Think 9/11, Covid, Putin, inflation, Taiwan, Kim Jong-un.

Have a plan but be nimble.

CHAPTER 3

CHAPTER 3

Agency Positioning Power

It's An Agency Positioning Jungle

It's an advertising, digital, design, branding, experiential, social, influencer, SEO, SEM, PR, ecommerce agency jungle out there. Imagine a client trying to find the right-fit agency resource to work with. I've been a client that bought agency services. It isn't an easy decision.

There are a lot of options. When I do a Google search on "advertising agency," I get 17.8 million results. When I search "digital agency," I get 20.3 million. "Media agency" yields 11.6 million.

Want even more potentially head-spinning numbers? IBISWorld reported that there are 7,865 businesses in the digital advertising agency industry. Clutch's database of advertising agencies lists 9,295 for New York, 2,552 for the UK, 272 for the United Arab Emirates, 1,095 in London, UK, and, get this, 105 in London, Ohio. Ohio!

Yikes.

CHAPTER 3

Regardless of what number you find and how you search, there are a lot of marketing services options for a client to choose from.

Distinction vs. Sameness

Help your future clients out a bit by creating brand differentiation and distinctive energy. Get past sameness.

Most agencies (and companies for that matter) have a me-too positioning, look, and brand messaging (especially the copy they use).

- Sameness makes it difficult to stand out and accelerate sales
- Sameness will be ignored
- Sameness does not power agency selection
- Sameness erodes profitability
- Distinction delivers a higher profit margin
- Distinctive agencies get bought

Everything you do should be judged on how much distinction you bring to the market.

We're eons into the advertising business and I cannot figure out why so many advertising agencies cannot create a unique sales proposition—or worse, don't seem to care about having one.

The Expert Agency

Al Reis was one of the leading branding gurus. His best-selling books include *The 22 Immutable Laws of Marketing*, *Positioning: The Battle for Your Mind*, and *Focus: The Future of Your Company Depends on It*.

Al has four key rules:
1. **Get focused.**
   Build or refocus your company around a singular idea. "When you try to be everything, you wind up being nothing."

2. **Act like a leader.**
   "What should a brand leader advertise? Brand leadership, of course. Leadership is the single most important motivating factor in consumer behavior."
3. **Have a battle cry.**
   Al's daughter Laura (yes, branding expertise runs in the family) pushes the idea of having a slogan. Works for brands, why not agencies? The slogan of New York's Mischief is "At No Fixed Address."
4. **Create one-word equity.**
   Here's a tough one. Can you own a word? Daniel Pink would like you to own a word. "I was thinking about the business implications of the Obama juggernaut the other day when a friend said to me, 'I can't think of the word "hope" any more without thinking of the guy.'"

My take is that clients want expertise and leadership. They want to know what you can do for them right now. Help them make the decision. Put yourself in their shoes.

Expert agencies break out from the universe of advertising-agency clutter.

Here is a break out agency.

eatbigfish: The Challenger Expert

eatbigfish and its challenger brand expertise and focus stand out from the pack.

Simply put, a challenger brand is not the industry leader.

eatbigfish owns the idea of challenger brands. They own the word *challenger.*

I like the idea of targeting challenger brands because it defines a target market for both the agency and clients.

Here is what the eatbigfish website says about their expertise. Note the term *strategic consultancy*, not *agency*.

We're a global strategic consultancy dedicated to challenger brands.

We're eatbigfish. And we know challenger brands better than anyone.

Whether you're a start-up or a global market leader, everyone can be more challenger.

eatbigfish supports their positioning via on-target thought leadership. This includes their annual *The Challengers to Watch* report and four books, including *Eating the Big Fish* and *Overthrow II: 10 Strategies from the New Wave of Challengers*. They also have dozens of branded videos on YouTube.

Being defined as the leading challenger-brand agency appears to work. eatbigfish works with rather large brands, including Google, Charles Schwab, HSBC, Audi, and KFC. Nice list.

Positioning Options

Brand positioning is the backbone of any marketing communications agency's business development program. Your positioning informs your business and marketing plans and positions you in the mind of clients so they can more easily decide that they want to talk and eventually work with you.

Agency positionings generally fall into one of these buckets:
- Skill based (branding, experiential, media expert, social media, SEM)
- Industry based (hospitality, health care, beverages)
- Target market based (B2C; B2B)
- Demographic based (Gen-X, Hispanics, seniors)

- Geographically based (local/regional expert)
- Strategic guru (brand strategy, research, insights)
- Creative genius (elegant problem solvers)
- Full-service ("We can do it all"—the one-stop shop)
- Creative consultancy (the übersmart marketing partner)

I know that the tighter an agency's positioning (and thus its sales proposition), the easier it is to attract the attention of a prospective client, agency search consultants, the press and, someday, a buyer.

The Elevator Pitch

I ask all my advertising agency clients to give me their agency's elevator pitch. I ask them to tell me what they do in eight seconds. Why eight seconds? A study by Microsoft Canada found that the average person has an attention span of about eight seconds. I ask my clients to deliver their positioning, sales proposition, and what they do as if we were in an elevator going up three floors.

One of my favorite super-expert positioning stories is about an agency that once *owned* the idea of mobile.

I was at New York's Advertising Week conference a few years ago. An agency exec invited me to go to the Soho Club for a drink. When we approached the bar, we needed to ask a guy to move over one seat so my drink mate and I could sit together. I asked the middle seat guy if he could move. As he shifted, I asked him if he was in New York for the conference. He said yes. I asked him what his agency did. He told me that his London-based Fetch was the leading mobile specialist.

It took him three seconds to deliver his expert positioning and elevator (or bar stool) pitch: "Fetch is the leading mobile agency."

By the way, Fetch Media Limited was purchased by Dentsu Aegis. Experts get bought. More on this later.

CHAPTER 3

CHAPTER 4

Marketing Starts Here

Nail These Big Three

When I build out business development plans for my clients, I always start with what I call the Big Three—the Big Three Musts.

Before you write your master business development plan, begin to create detailed inbound and account-based marketing programs. Start here.

If you don't get these three business development elements right… fuhgeddaboudit.

My must dos.

Make Sure Your Agency Is Findable

Make sure you are where people are looking for your type of agency. Let's say a major health-care client is looking for a health-care marketing

CHAPTER 4

specialist just like you. Will they find you in their search? If not, you are invisible.

Invisible does not work well when a potentially hot lead is looking for your agency's skills and expertise.

Put your client hat on and ask, "Where and how would I find a company like mine?"

Start here. Are you everywhere a client might look?

- Are you on the first page of a relevant Google or Bing search? A tough objective. If you're not listed there, audit and activate your SEO plan. Consider testing an ad to get on that first page. Find a message that breaks through the clutter.
- Are you listed in all related marketing services directories? Clutch? Agency Spotter? Winmo? The Manifest? Clients use these.
- Is you brand optimized on creative source websites like Behance or Dribble?
- Are you on your regional or national agency club or organization lists?
- Do you optimize your LinkedIn presence? Do you review and manage all leadership and key employee profiles? Do you regularly post on LinkedIn?
- Do the major search consultants know you're alive? They want to know you—it's their job. I have a list of all advertising agency search firms on my blog. It gets serious traffic.
- Do you win awards? Being listed on the right award websites (from Webby Awards to Adweek's Best to AAF) is a good thing, a very good thing. Awards = awareness = third-party blessing = client interest.
- Do you attend and speak at marketing and client-industry conferences? Write for industry publications to build out your authority?
- Do you have a managed brand that positions you as a category expert? Does the industry press know you're a go-to category expert who's always ready to give an educated sound bite?

- If you are a solo resource (or a creative director looking for a side hustle), are you on Upwork and Behance?

Note that you will never be alone in a search for marketing specialists, so strive to be unignorable when you get found. Be that valuable expert.

Make this an ongoing question: Are you everywhere a client might look for an agency like yours?

Goose Referrals

It seems that all agencies say they get most of their new clients from positive referrals. It is the default. This is especially true in geographic or defined-category markets where a personal recommendation is common.

This is great. Be proactive about getting referred.

A key to having a robust referral strategy is to make sure that your current and past clients are aware that you want referrals. Getting referrals from happy customers is one of best ways B2B companies generate new business. Not a huge surprise. However, what is surprising is how few companies have a dedicated strategy for growing these valuable referrals.

Referrals lead as a sales generator for a couple of reasons: A referral is a white-hot lead. If we assume your happy customers are savvy enough to recommend you to the right potential customer, then you are well on your way to establishing a valuable conversation and a new business win.

Most marketing services companies do not run highly effective sales programs, so the most effective new business tool is by default referrals.

Three Wonderful Benefits of Referrals
1. The closing ratio for referrals is high. It has been reported that the closing ratio of a referral is six times greater than for a potentially unqualified lead.
2. For the obvious reason that a referred prospect is generally a very motivated buyer, the referral-generated sales cycle can be as much as 75% shorter.

3. A referral strategy is cost-effective and will reduce your sales expenditures. Less expensive is good.

Six Effective "Active" Referral Strategies

I've generated referrals from existing clients and customers using the following set of strategies.
1. Start with an objective. Know what type of clients you want.
2. Determine which of your clients or friends might know the people or businesses on your prospect list.
3. Be proactive—go ahead and ask for referrals. Some referrals come because your client or buddy is specifically asked if they know of a good company in your business category. Some come because your customers love you so much, they actively "sell" you. Most need to be stimulated to think about how to help you.
4. Make it easy for people to refer you. Think incentives. Yes, a monetary offer like an Amazon gift card is kosher. Say "thank you" twice.
5. Make sure a potential referrer knows how to talk about you and your brilliant expert positioning.
6. This is not a one-time shot. Consider reminding your friends about your offer quarterly. Gently. Can you make this fun? Sure.

Referrals are nice, but one eventually runs out of friends with friends. How do you deal with this unfortunate fact? Yes, do marketing. Even stimulate internal marketing to existing clients.

Focus on Client Retention and Growth

The most efficient, stress efficient business development strategy is growth from current clients. Like for referrals, an agency needs to have a clear client retention and growth strategy.
- This should not be random. Do not leave it up to untrained

account people. Have a conscious retention and growth system.
- Hug your clients. Give them new ideas. Challenge them. Deliver smart growth proposals. Nicely. A key reason clients walk out the door is that the agency is not idea driven. Be a relevant thought leader.
- If it is project account, make sure you have a preplanned agency plan on how to present new ideas and agency services. Not a list but a strategic approach to how to sell-in relevant services that will excite and create dialogue. These could be productized services like a branded SEM program.

The delivery of superior customer service is the rule here. Do not upsell—be value driven and upserve. Yes, upserve.

From Daniel Pink: "Anytime you're tempted to upsell someone else, stop what you're doing and upserve instead."

I discuss the idea of upserving in greater detail in Chapter 19, "The Savvy Account Manager."

CHAPTER 4

CHAPTER 5

Please Be Unignorable

Thank You, john st.

OK, once you've settled on a clear and compelling brand position, a unique sales proposition, ask, how will your message stand out from the pack?

You need to be unignorable.

Building an unignorable agency brand and voice is a critical element in my agency business development philosophy. Your agency can run down the business development checklist: inbound marketing—check; outbound account-based marketing—check; a sweet LinkedIn profile, the cool website, a YouTube channel—check; lots of wonderful thought leadership—check.

But if all of that is ignorable in a saturated agency-selection environment, you lose.

I discovered the power word *unignorable* when I took a hard look at

CHAPTER 5

Toronto's agency john st.

john st. built the idea of being unignorable into their agency ethos. From the john st. website:

> Be unignorable.
>
> Our mission is to make our clients' brands unignorable. We use insight, analytics, intuition and sweat to do it. But we mostly use sweat.

Unignorable is their focus—their expertise. Clients want to be unignorable; john st. delivers.

Unignorable is the agency's one-word equity. They own it.

Unignorable is a distinctive battle cry. I haven't seen one other agency use this word.

Want to see john st. in action? Look at the agency's YouTube channel—videos that act as john st.'s brand drivers and are unquestionably unignorable.

Their "Catvertising" video has 2.4+ million views. MILLION! "Buyral" has 1 million views. Does any other agency have this many video views? No.

john st.'s creative director told me that these videos drove incoming queries from brands like Coke. The Coke question was, "Whoa, who are you guys?"

john st.'s dedication to being unignorable and creating unignorable work for clients was a factor in their being acquired by WPP.

Getting to Unignorable

You need to be unignorable to get past being ignored. The world of marketing services is too large and... most agencies sound alike. Oy... and look and feel alike.

Here are eight paths to being unignorable:
1. Make the decision to break out. Like, decide to be refreshingly different.
2. Use unignorable personality and tone. It's OK to build an unignorable personality. Check out Chapter 7, "You Inc.," which deals with personal branding and how to craft your standout persona.
3. Understand the intellectual and emotional needs of your market. Grab them by the mind *and* heart.
4. Have a must-read and must-listen-to POV. *Must-read* means that you are offering your market something of undeniable value. My website's list of advertising awards consistently delivers mega traffic to my blog.
5. Be known for something. For example, build and brand a quarterly study that positions you as a leader in your category.
6. Be ubiquitous. Put your thinking on LinkedIn and YouTube and TikTok and speak at the right conferences. Have a PR plan. Do something that *Campaign* magazine can't ignore. They need to fill up those issues.
7. Get a face on. Put a face on the agency. OK, not all bosses can be a handsome David Droga. But many could be but are not out in front of the agency brand. Remember that clients buy both expertise and personality. Interpersonal chemistry is often the deciding factor. Why not start being human on your website?
8. Be funny. Humor works. I used a Cameo impersonator to create "I love Peter" Trump, Gandhi, and Borat promotional videos for my consultancy. The Borat video was so well done that I've had people ask me how I got the *real* Borat to make the video.

Remember, there are hundreds, if not thousands, of marketing service firms that a marketing client can choose from. Standing out from the pack is critical.

CHAPTER 5

CHAPTER 6
Thought Leadership

Thinking Works

In 2018 Ford Motor Company left long-term agency WPP for BBDO. A big move like this was big news, of course. But more interesting to me was Ford's hiring of Wieden+Kennedy New York as its "innovation agency."

Ford was looking to W+K to uncover new approaches, creative approaches, and to resolve marketplace issues and opportunities.

Being an innovation agency is a valuable business development tool. Here's a 2022 *Adweek* headline: "Ford Picks Wieden+Kennedy as Its Global Agency Partner for Creative and Brand Strategy." Apparently four years of W+K's dedicated role as Ford's innovation agency helped it to land the full account.

Clients large and small want and need marketing advice and brains. Given the speed of change and transformation, clients need advice about how to wrestle with our ever-changing marketing universe. Today, many clients are wondering how AI will affect marketing. Help them think through this future.

Thought Leadership Is Good

The marketing term *thought leadership* has become a bit of overused jargon. Well, what marketing term is not a bit overused? I mean, do I really want to hear the word *disruption* again and again?

However, if we step back a bit and ask ourselves if we'd like to be perceived as an insightful, strategic, and creative thinker—um… a thought leader—well, I'll take the words *thought leader*.

Thought leaders deliver actionable
- information
- insights
- strong opinions
- inspiration
- creativity
- innovation
- even peace of mind

Since I started my consultancy, I have produced more than 850 blog posts and some videos (I'll admit not quite as sharp as "Catvertising"), have been a host and a guest on dozens of podcasts, and have spoken at conferences and produced white papers. I've recently launched a LinkedIn newsletter.

I wrote my book on pitching (still selling well) and this book on advertising agency management. Books generate interest and proof of expertise.

My thought leadership, which is 100% dedicated to advertising agency management and business development, works. Specialization works.

The benefits of thought leadership are clear:

- It demonstrates expertise and authority.
- It delivers compelling, relevant business-building information and insights. Value!
- It excites.
- It generates peer-to-peer conversations and builds relationships over time.
- It generates marketing-qualified leads.
- It can be amplified and repurposed for efficiency. One thought can be modified and spread over a range of distribution platforms.
- Kick-ass thought leadership is unignorable.

Thinking Is Tough Work

Thought leadership isn't easy.

I'm laughing as I write this. You'll need to start with compelling thoughts, a degree of leadership, and the right authors.

Ashley Faus, the director of integrated product marketing at Atlassian, lists four pillars of a successful thought leadership program:

1. Credibility—unquestioned knowledge and authority. Have an opinion.
2. Profile—a big, known company or a title.
3. Being prolific—publishing ongoing long- and short-form content across multiple channels.
4. Delivering depth—producing new ideas, strategies, methods, and actional tactics.

To get to the promised land, you'll need an ongoing content development production system and a content program calendar.

Consistency is critical. People and algorithms have short memories.

A thought leadership program needs the right people to manage the program (harder for smaller agencies than larger) and dedication, as in a strong commitment, from the top.

One more big piece of advice: I'd start with a thought leadership creative brief. Define your objectives and audience, their needs, and how you will deliver that wonderful thinking.

The Unignorable Insight

Your expert positioning will drive thought leadership, and that power word is *authority*. Market-building insights are created and delivered via your knowledge, experience, and creative approach to problem solving.

Just what is an insight? From the Planning Dirty Academy's Julian Cole: "Insight unlocks the way around a problem. It reveals a new path."

Problem + Solution

Not every client you target will be receptive to your fabulous, intriguing, and business-building insight. But I have always thought that the client who responds to my crafted and targeted insights is the client who deserves to work with me. How's that for rationalization?

Building Insights

According to Brent Dykes in *Forbes*,

> Insights are generated by analyzing information and drawing conclusions. Both data and information set the stage for the discovery of insights that can then influence decisions and drive change.

Brent goes beyond the simple delivery of an insight to what he calls data storytelling. Storytelling breeds interest and is, yes, unignorable.

Like any marketing campaign, your thought leadership program needs a plan.

Six Insight Thought Starters

1. What are your business objectives? What does success look like?
2. Who is your target audience? Business owners, CMOs, marketing staff, CEOs, even CFOs? How do they consume information?
3. What are their issues? What keeps them up at night? What do they want from an advertising agency: strategic thinking, new packaging or just some SEO, please?
4. What strategic or tactical thinking and what specific subjects should you address? Do the research. What trends could use some of your polished thinking? Google Alerts is a real-time info tool to help you stay on top of a trend, category, or brand.
5. Perform the competitive analysis to see what your agency competition is doing. Look at their thought leadership materials. If it looks like they've found an insight sweet spot, then look at how you can leverage that information. Can you do it better?
6. What information gaps can you fill? Be strategic.

Idea: Why not brand and productize your thought leadership program? Stand apart. Make your perspective sound smart.

Stealing Ideas

Need ideas? One of my favorite books is Austin Kleon's *Steal Like an Artist. 10 Things Nobody Told You About Being Creative.*

The idea here is that there is already great thinking out there and not a lot of really new ideas. Why not steal from and massage elements from the idea universe?

Your very own secret sauce is your point of view and hard-to-ignore opinion. Strong opinions rock.

Are you worried about idea or subject theft? Take it, Picasso: "Art is theft." How about David Bowie? "The only art I will ever study is stuff that I can steal from." Even more theft from a genius. Take it, Einstein:

CHAPTER 6

"The secret to creativity is knowing how to hide your sources."

I'm not suggesting that you steal and simply regurgitate other people's thought leadership ideas. But, as I mentioned above, studying your competition and industry gurus will generate some thought kernels.

18 Insight Tools

New strategic tools that generate insights roll out every month. Tools I use include:

1. Google Trends. Chances are good that you're aware of Google Trends. This a powerful tool to help you know what's hot and what's not in Google's search universe.
2. Think with Google—a free repository of Google data and research.
3. Google Alerts. Keep up with news related to an individual client or category.
4. Google Keyword Planner. Yes, more Google. From Google: You can use Keyword Planner to get insights into how keywords might perform. Google draws on historical search data to make estimates on what you might get from a set of keywords based on your spending.
5. AnswerThePublic. This is a free visual search listening tool that shows you what questions and queries your consumers have by getting a free report of what they're searching for on Google.
6. Exploding Topics. Yes, just like it sounds—a way to get to the next big idea. And get ahead of your competitors.
7. Quora—a top 100 website. All answers.
8. LivingFacts—how Americans live today from the PEW Research Center.
9. Statista—statistics and market research data.
10. vidIQ. Got a YouTube channel? From Backlinko: vidIQ is a SaaS product designed to help YouTube creators find topic and

keywords for their videos.
11. Social Mention. Ever wonder what the world is saying about you or your company? Here you go.
12. Buzzsumo. Buzzsumo analyzes over 8 billion articles. Enter a keyword and voila.
13. Sympler. Use their custom qualitative social media research.
14. SurveyMonkey, Typeform, and Qualaroo. Collect your very own market research data. Clients dig polls, even man-on-the-street interviews.
15. Ubersuggest. Unlock those effective competitive keywords and search trends.
16. Add PDF to a Google search query. You'll often find higher-level thinking, as in academic, on most subjects.
17. Gartner—insights and reports.
18. Search on a subject, say Instagram, and add the name of a trusted journal, like *The New Yorker* or *The Economist* and scan their headlines for smart insights. Thank you, Julian Cole, for this idea—a fast way to get to expert opinions.

Moving forward, many of us will let the latest AI tool do the analysis and you will then put your own spin on it.

CHAPTER 7

CHAPTER 7

You Inc.

Only You Own You

Back to marketing world clutter. "There are 7,761 Digital Advertising Agencies businesses in the US as of 2022, an increase of 17.4% from 2021" (IBISWorld). An increase of 17%. Wow.

Man, it's hard to break out when so many agencies are selling similar offers that sound alike.
- We are creative.
- Check out our SEO action plan.
- We'll build out your influencer network.
- We are a branding agency.

However, the something that your agency and you personally own big time is YOU.

Every advertising agency search consultant I've talked to about the agency selection process points to personality, as in interpersonal chemistry, as being a major factor in zeroing in on an agency when so many agencies kinda sound alike.

"I like you" is a powerful decision-making attribute. How will you be liked? Like your expert positioning, being well liked can be managed.

Your Personal Brand and Business

What is a personal brand? There are many definitions. I went to the website PersonalBrand.com for this definition (why not go to a company smart enough to have bought the URL PersonalBrand.com?):

> A personal brand is a widely-recognized and largely-uniform perception or impression of an individual based on their experience, expertise, competencies, actions and/or achievements within a community, industry, or the marketplace at large.

Kind of wordy but you get the idea.

I'm keen on the idea of building and managing a personal brand for agency leaders and senior managers. Your personal brand is how you present and control your image to your market—your current and potential clients, your competition, and your staff (and importantly, these days, your future staff.)

Advertising's Personal Masters

David Ogilvy

As I discuss in Chapter 23, "How to Build, Buy, and Sell an Agency," many agencies are named after their founder. In most of these cases, the founder is the face of the agency. The founder embodies the mission and soul of the agency.

Ogilvy the agency continues to use the brand essence of its founder David Ogilvy, who passed away in 1999. On its Careers page, the agency quotes David and leverages his personal brand to help sell the agency's soul to future employees:

> As our founder David Ogilvy put it, we seek people who are bigger and smarter than ourselves. That's how we create a company of giants. We're always looking for modern marketing and brand experts with big hearts and enormous talent.

How's that for branding? In 1962, *Time* magazine called Ogilvy "the most sought-after wizard in today's advertising industry." Believe me, this recognition did not happen by accident. Ogilvy was a brand image master.

The 1985 *Ogilvy on Advertising* continues to be one of the best-selling advertising books. Forty years on. Now that's personal branding, baby.

Mary Wells

Being a special first can drive a personal brand.

Mary Wells was the most famous woman in advertising in the 1960s and 1970s at a time when the business was considered a man's world. There were few, if any, Donna Drapers.

Better stated, Mary was one of the most famous *people* in adverting full-stop during those years.

Mary was a copywriter and co-founder of the agency Wells, Rich, Greene. WRG was universally known for its creativity at a time when building a brand's creative story, and taglines, ruled the industry. Mary's innovative campaigns included Alka Seltzer ("Plop, Plop, Fizz, Fizz" and "I Can't Believe I Ate the Whole Thing"), the Ford Motor Company ("Quality Is Job One"), BIC ("Flick Your Bic") and New York City's iconic ("I Love New York"). Five of the most effective campaigns of those years. Maybe ever.

Need more? Mary took WRG public in 1968, she became the first female CEO of a company traded on the New York Stock Exchange. She is in Advertising Hall of Fame.

Hello Gary Vaynerchuck

Gary Vaynerchuck is arguably the most ubiquitous personal brand in today's advertising industry. He is the chairman of New York–based communications company VaynerX and is CEO of VaynerMedia. VaynerMedia is number five on *Ad Age*'s 2022 Agency A-List.

No single person in the advertising industry works their personal brand harder than Gary. His brand reminds me of James Brown's reputation as being the hardest-working man in show business.

Gary's energy is boundless.

His Twitter feed, @garyvee, has 3.1 million followers—and get this, over 208,000 tweets. All growing daily. Interestingly, he follows close to 20,000 Twitter accounts, including me. Loving back is a good thing.

His NFT project @veefriends has over 258,000 followers.

Gary's LinkedIn profile has 5.2 million followers. His YouTube channel has 3.9 million subs, and he produces eight-ish videos a day. A day.

Gary's personal brand is brash, intelligent, hyperactive, smart, and so prescient that it sells his agency every day.

This dude is committed. It helps that he has a branding and content staff backing him up.

The David Droga Journey

The David Droga brand, and its Droga5 agency, is all about creativity. It's an agency that nailed its creative positioning.

Droga leveraged his high-visibility position (and award-winning expertise) as regional creative director of Saatchi Asia to have it named

Media Marketing's Asia Regional Network of the Year. *Ad Age* named the Singapore office International Agency of the Year. After moving to London, Saatchi & Saatchi London won Global Agency of the Year at the Cannes International Advertising Festival.

This was not an accident. Lots of agencies are cool, but Droga just might be the ultimate heavy lifter of pumping awards for fame and fortune.

This guy is a master at building his own brand to help build Droga5. He built his agency to a point where it was purchased by Accenture in 2019 for around $475 million. Accenture bought the agency's client roster, talent, and, yes, the brand. Oh, and David.

The Stan Richards Downside

There can be a personal brand downside. Yikes: the Richards Group.

Having an agency associated with its founder can be a negative. From *Adweek,*

> In October, news leaked that in an internal meeting for longtime client Motel 6, Richards, who at nearly 90 years old remained actively involved with the company, referred to a campaign idea for the client as being "too Black" and *implied that some of Motel 6's customers were white supremacists.* (emphasis added)

The agency quickly lost four major accounts: Motel 6, Keurig Dr Pepper, Salvation Army, and H-E-B.

Stan Richards was 90, for Pete's sake. Yet his own brand was fully tied to that of the agency. He *and* his agency got cancelled during the height of cancel culture.

Ann Handley vs. McCann

Can a one-person personal branding machine beat the brand of a mega

CHAPTER 7

advertising agency? An agency born in 1902. Yes.

Ann Handley is a personal branding super force. Interesting stat:

> McCann New York has 477 employees and 87,993 LinkedIn followers. Ann Handley has 458,506 followers.

From Ann's bio:

> Ann Handley is a Wall Street Journal bestselling author who speaks worldwide about how businesses can escape marketing mediocrity to ignite tangible results. IBM named her one of the 7 people shaping modern marketing. Ann is a digital marketing pioneer and the Chief Content Officer of MarketingProfs, the leading marketing training company with more than 600,000 subscribers.

How did she make it? Ann has written for Entrepreneur magazine, IBM's Think Marketing, Inc. magazine, Mashable, Huffington Post, American Express, NPR, and the Wall Street Journal.

Her best sellers include *Everybody Writes: Your Go-To Guide to Creating Ridiculously Good Content*, and co-author of *Content Rules: How to Create Killer Blogs, Podcasts, Videos, Ebooks, Webinars (and More) That Engage Customers and Ignite Your Business*.

If you or your agency needs some help being a writer (and a social media hero), check her out.

What about You?

Today our personal brand is out there for all to see. We are on LinkedIn, on our website's About page, in cute Instagram posts, in our new books.

Whether an agency leader wants to become as famous as David Droga or not, they most often have no choice. The market might just brand them whether they like it or not. The key is to control it.

There are three core elements to how to build and control a leadership brand.

1. **Prioritize your branding.**

    Define your area of expertise, your persona, and what you want to be known for. Be authentic and an authority.

    Think through your story framework.

    Pay close attention to your client and prospect personas and their needs. Some might want Gary's chutzpah. Some might find it off-putting.

2. **Be ubiquitous and consistent.**

    Optimize your presence. Start with your website. How are you presented? If you're a good actor or communicator, why not star in the agency video? Make sure your LinkedIn profile is well written. And keep it going because we are in that voracious 360-degree + 24/7 universe.

3. **Be visible.**

    If you want fame, have a plan for how and where you will deliver your personal brand story. Your plan will help you select the right media. If you have a face for radio (as the old joke goes) then do a podcast. If you're a good writer, consider writing a book. Good speaker? Then go after speaking engagements. Do you look and sound impressive? Then go video.

Team Branding... Too

Everyone in your agency has a personal brand, whether they manage it or not.

Over 700 employees at Droga5 have LinkedIn profiles. Each of their

CHAPTER 7

profiles adds to (or subtracts) from the master Droga5 brand. Many of these people have 200 or more connections (some way more.) Many are active on LinkedIn, posting and reposting and liking other people's posts.

If we do some estimating, it's quite possible that these 700 Droga5ers have a LinkedIn reach of over 140,000 connections. That's 700 Droga5ers times 200 connections. This reach could generate mega views of an agency news item.

Do these people's own brand add to the brand value of the total agency? Do they help or hurt the brand? I suggest that for at least very senior management, any agency look at how they are presented in social media. Why not a LinkedIn profile audit?

No, I am not suggesting that you form a social media personal brand police force. I'm just saying that how your people are presented to the world will reflect on your agency brand. It is all additive, every day.

I looked at Droga5's head of business development profile on LinkedIn, since this position drives outbound communications and is, in many cases, the first point of contact for a prospective new client.

Pat Rowley gets his brand right. It supports the agency's creative positioning. Some copy from his "About" section:

> Strategic business leader, highly motivated to help ambitious brands achieve meaningful growth—through fostering collaborative partnerships and driving purposeful, effective work.
>
> Impressive portfolio and experience over a wide range of categories for leading global brands in the US, Australia/New Zealand and Asia. Recognized for over 30 major effectiveness and creative awards at the shows that matter most (Effies, Cannes, D&AD) as part of collaborative teams at the world's top agencies.

This isn't a random set of attributes. Pat is managing his brand. Brand as marketing tool. Not a brand-new idea.

"The Brand Called You"

A bit of early you-branding history. Tom Peters' 1997 *Fast Company* article "The Brand Called You" was the first time the marketing world began to think about the effectiveness of managing one's personal brand. Here is the article's subhead:

> Big companies understand the importance of brands. Today, in the Age of the Individual, you have to be your own brand. Here's what it takes to be the CEO of Me Inc.

I'll bet that Mr. Vaynerchuck knows he is the CEO of his Me.

Some thoughts on how to get to your very own Me Inc:
1. The first step is to know how you want to be perceived. Hey, it is branding after all.
2. Build out and sell-in your expertise.
3. Establish your own brand voice.
4. Aim to be unignorable. One path is to be opinionated.
5. Be authentic. Yes, that word again.
6. Build out your personal story. Gary went from selling wine in his dad's store, to doing online wine reviews in the early days of YouTube to being known as a king of social media.

A caveat: This personal branding work can be a component of personal overwork burnout. Once again, the idea of "Keep it simple, stupid!" should be considered. Gary has a staff to get his Me out there.

That said, get out there.

Six Branding Platforms

1. Personal Video

Australian Tiny Hunter's video program kicks ass. The agency's Jodi de

CHAPTER 7

Vries, Jo Gossage, Kiri White and Emma Scott sell-in the agency brand, culture, and personality. Their short form *Branding Before Breakfast* averages about two minutes per episode. Thank you, Tiny Hunter, for respecting my time.

Past titles include "A Brand Competitor Review Framework," "Slice and Dice: Maximize and Amplify Your Content," and "The 90-Day Rule: The Importance of Brand Storytelling."

Watch the videos. It doesn't get more personal than this. Jodi, Jo, Kiri, and Emma are the agency brand. I like them. I'd want to work with them.

2. Branding by the Book

Should you write a book to help sell your personal and advertising agency brand? Clearly, considering you're reading *my* book (and considering its inherent Me-branding objective), my answer is yes. Writing a book delivers

- Credibility—proof that you are an expert (and a creative thinker).
- Visibility—marketing a book helps you and your agency to break out from the me-too clutter. My The Levitan Pitch book got me speaking engagements at HubSpot's Inbound conference (where I discussed how to write an agency book), and talks at the 4 A's, and ANA. Plus, lots of print and podcast interviews.
- Marketing and lead generation—use the book, and importantly excerpts, to drive blog posts, newsletter sign-ups, and LinkedIn contacts. Go direct and send the book to your most cherished prospects and influencers.
- PR action—the media (trade press, podcasters, conferences) need interesting new content. Books rise to the top.

Thirteen steps to get a book written and distributed:
1. Have objectives. What's the point of all of this work? Fill in the blanks: I am writing this book because _____. My book's

audience is _____. They will read it because _____.
2. Have an unignorable subject. Meld your insights, advice, and guidance with a bit of storytelling. A touch of attitude plus humor helps. Ask, how can I make this book so valuable and unignorable for a select audience that they must read it?
3. Study the existing market. Where will the book fit in and be competitive? Do the research.
4. Develop an outline and start writing. Write every day. Be dedicated.
5. Work with an editor. There are two types: a developmental or content editor (they will work with you on your subject matter) and a copy editor. No typos please. I hope.
6. Create a power title and descriptive subtitle. How could we resist the title *The Four-Hour Work Week*? Or *How to Win Friends and Influence People*? Mark Manson's title *The Subtle Art of Not Giving a F*ck* is hard to resist.
7. Design a cover that stands out. While you'd love to be in that airport bookstore, you'll probably sell most books on Amazon, where your cover will be seen as a thumbnail graphic.
8. A *big* decision: Should you self-publish or find a traditional publisher? My advice for what is most likely your B2B lead-gen book is to go the self-published route. Working with traditional book publishers, unless you are Oprah or Seth or Malcolm, is a pain in the ass, is a very slow process, and really, do *you* really expect to sell a specialized B2B book at Barnes & Noble or an airport bookstore?
9. Control costs. The cost to design and print is minimal, especially if you work at an advertising agency. You have designers, copywriters, smart marketers, and Amazon profile generators in house. Your biggest cost will be your time.
10. Planning and process. Make the book a priority. Deadlines work. Have a well-tooled editorial and marketing plan and timetable.
11. Pricing. It's free to publish a print-on-demand book on Amazon

through their online Kindle Direct Publishing platform. There are no upfront costs. Amazon will take a portion of your book's earnings to print, leaving you with 60% royalties after the book's print price. Frankly, so what. This book won't be a big money maker. My *The Levitan Pitch* has paid for itself and more via sales and business leads. Consider selling at a lower price to encourage more sales and therefore more reviews.

12. Manage Amazon. This includes optimizing the descriptive copy for you and your book, adding a video, selecting the right keywords and categorization, getting reviewed (ask people early), and pricing the book to sell. Consider advertising on Amazon (and beyond).
13. Market the heck out of it. Start marketing ahead of publication (like build your email list). Add book marketing to your company website and build a standalone landing page. Send the book to prospects, the press, influencers. Leverage your network. Find new friends via LinkedIn Navigator. Seek speaking and guest podcasting opportunities. Repurpose the copy and point back to the book. In 2023, create short videos.

I believe the key here is to really want to get the book published. Sounds obvious, right?

3. Podcasting Is Personal

Podcasting is intimate. Podcasts make personal connections. Podcasting is a virtual story platform. Podcasting builds a fan base.

There are way fewer podcasts than blogs. I could stop with this statement, but the numbers speak rather loudly: 2.4 million podcasts (DemandSage, June 2022) versus 600 million blogs (EarthWeb, November 2022).

Podcasting works for agencies. Neil Patel and Eric Sui's *Marketing School* podcast has over 70 million downloads. They've built their digital agencies by delivering daily short-form advice. Douglas Burdette's *The Marketing Book Podcast*, at over 400 episodes, builds awareness of his Sales Artillery agency. Drew McLellan's *Build A Better Agency* podcast builds his consultancy. I mention him because I have been a guest on the show twice and it has driven my leads.

Yes, there are some issues to resolve. I know about them, as I launched my first agency podcast in 2007 and did my limited *Advertising Stories* series during the pandemic.

Podcasting takes time and dedication to get traction.

Priscilla McKinney of Little Bird Marketing is the gold standard for ad agency podcast marketing. First, she is consistent and has published more than 300 episodes. Imagine how much energy and time this has taken.

Priscilla built a comprehensive podcast marketing program that includes self-promotion that supports every high-quality podcast Priscilla does. She creates a transcript and converts the show into a blog post landing page, videos, LinkedIn posts, graphical tweets, and outbound emails.

Plus, she does guest stimulation (as in she gets her guests to promote her show—and deliver backlinks to her website). Priscilla also runs a mutual admiration society. I've been on her show, and she has been on mine.

All this production effort takes staff time. Staff time costs money. Do it right and it pays off.

Be patient.

I've already mentioned the time it takes to create and publish a great podcast series. Here is one more timing issue: It takes a very long time to build an audience.

Be prepared to go the distance. And be prepared to not be discouraged. Buzzsprout has published these download numbers that show just how hard it is to be popular. Yikes.

New episode facts:
- More than 26 downloads, you're in the top 50% of podcasts.

- More than 72 downloads, you're in the top 25% of podcasts.
- More than 231 downloads, you're in the top 10% of podcasts.
- More than 539 downloads, you're in the top 5% of podcasts.
- More than 3,062 downloads, you're in the top 1% of podcasts.

By the way, and unsurprisingly, most of the top podcasts that will eat up your potential downloads are produced by pro publishers like NPR, Gimlet, Spotify, The New York Times, and iHeartRadio. In the advertising world, you'll compete with shows from Adweek, Campaign, Ad Age, and the Drum.

Think about pet care.

Think hard before you commit to doing a podcast. Podcasting is like owning a dog. You need to feed it and walk it. A lot.

You will need time plus a quality show plus the right audience goal plus perseverance.

Podfade is where a show just stops. I'm not talking about a limited series (not a bad idea—it's what I did), but a show that just stops dead in its tracks.

Think about the possibility that you might succumb to podfade when you start to plan your show. Be prepared to market around it.

Set realistic expectations. Maybe just start with a clearly targeted series or a seasonal format. Why not a ten-part series on summer travel for the hospitality industry?

I've included a sample podcasting Creative Brief in Resources.

4. A More Efficient Idea: Be a Podcast Guest

Being a guest on an established show just might be a savvy alternative to producing your own podcast. Podcast guesting is like having a speaking gig at a large industry conference.

Every show out there needs guests.

I have probably been on over 40 shows. The right shows will generate awareness and positive personal branding—and good news, you don't have to do the heavy lifting. You get the show's audience and their marketing chutzpah.

I tested the services of Tom Schwab's Interview Valet to get me on the right shows through strategic appearances. They did the heavy lifting—the outbound talent marketing—for me. Visit the Interview Valet website for mucho guesting insights. Tell him I sent you. He is a connector.

5. TikTok… And… Um

Need another personal brand platform? Don't answer that. Just stay with me.

In addition to driving personal branding à la the Vaynerchuck all-in be-everywhere universe model, podcasting, and writing books, you could start a TikTok channel. TikTok is currently a wide open B2B playing field.

Note that I am assuming that Congress hasn't killed TikTok. If it does, there will be, should be, a new app to take its place.

Ashley Rutstein, a Denver freelance creative director, did just that. Her TikTok channel *Stuff About Advertising* (@stuffaboutadvertising) has over 45,000 followers. Forty+ K!

Ashley's TikTok video "A Few of the Agencies Out There 'Doing It Right" has 1,325 likes. She mentions a list of agencies and points to Mischief's TikTok channel, which includes a video on their winning a Cannes Lion. Yes, folks, awards and TikTok equal smart personal and agency branding.

In addition to TikTok we now have YouTube Shorts and Instagram Reels. Hard to know where this short world is going. Yet regardless of the platform, short videos are kicking it.

6. Awards Are Personal

Winning advertising awards will elevate your brand. Accepting the award puts you and your agency in the spotlight.

CHAPTER 7

Clients include awards in their searches. They need that third-party imprimatur.

A totally rough look at Google Trends suggests that there are over 15,000 searches on "advertising awards" every year. There are another 15,000-plus searches for "ad awards." While I bet that most of these searches are made by advertising agency people, the number of searches on awards-related keywords is high.

Put yourself in a marketing client's shoes. They want to find and select a new advertising, digital, or design firm. How do they do that?

They ask friends, spend hours searching the internet. Perhaps they were directly targeted by an agency's account-based marketing, read an agency's thought leadership, or hired an agency search consultant. Regardless, finding the right agency in the sea of agencies isn't easy.

Many clients look at advertising and design award winners to find an agency. Third-party recognition is a client aphrodisiac.

The Benefits of Winning

1. Fame is good. The fame equation is simple: Advertising awards drive global and local industry awareness of an agency. You get something new and shiny to talk about. If it is a big award, you can put it on your home page.
2. Your existing clients receive confirmation that they made the right decision when they hired you. Some might even congratulate you.
3. Your agency staff feels good. Their work is being recognized. They are working at the right agency.
4. You'll use the award in your recruitment program.
5. You'll have a statuette to put in your award-strewn agency reception area. Assuming you still have an office.

OK. Do it.

Across my global and regional advertising career, my agency groups won big creative awards like the One Show, marketing success awards including a bunch of Effies, and regional ad awards like the American Advertising Awards from the AAF.

You could even go for client-industry awards. My Oregon agency won the best marketing award from the American Bankers Association for work we did for a regional bank. We beat out the Bank of Americas and JB Morgan Chases of the universe. We leveraged this award to initiate talks with other financial clients.

Build an Award Marketing Plan

It's mind-blowing how many advertising agencies don't know how to enter an award show to win.

Too many agencies don't approach the award process with a plan or objectives beyond the search for ego fulfillment. This can make the whole effort a bit too C R A Z Y. You know that.

The horror! Too many agencies deliver poorly written me-too award entries. Consider the judges and their mindset. They must read dozens of award entries. How will you break out of the clutter to nail that award?

Too many entries sound alike: entries that are not creative, entries with typos, and agencies that do not know how to craft a case study. Worse, agencies do not seem to understand the award-judge audience and do not approach entry writing via strategic thinking.

Go out and enter the right award shows. Be strategic. Be unignorable.

I have a list of all advertising awards on my blog. A very well-read post.

CHAPTER 8

CHAPTER 8
Intellectual Property

Basecamp and Money

I want you to close your eyes... Well, no, keep them open and just think about this.

History. Way back in 2004 the agency 37signals had a need for a smart, easy-to-use project management tool, was not enamored with existing solutions, and decided to build their own solution for the agency.

Basecamp delivered to-do lists, milestone management, forum-like messaging, file sharing, and time tracking.

Agency clients and other agencies began using the tool, and within a month Basecamp had over 100 paying customers. Today over 20 million people have used Basecamp.

Even more IP. Basecamp itself is moving forward. It launched Hey, an email service, in June 2020.

Need a smile? 37signals dumped its agency business and went

full-time into its SaaS service. Its intellectual property was more valuable that its service business—and, I bet, after the initial investment, an easier path to profits. Could you and your agency follow this path?

IP and Growth

This chapter covers two growth areas that I think every agency needs to consider: owning intellectual property and owning a product.

Be an Owner

A way out of the *all agencies sound alike* maze is to develop and own intellectual property. You might not be able to own the amorphous idea of creativity, but you can own IP.

From the Oxford Dictionary:
> Intellectual property is a work or invention that is the result of creativity, such as a manuscript or a design, to which one has rights and for which one may apply for a patent, copyright, trademark, etc.

To get past the legalese, I prefer to call intellectual property intellectual equity. Equity as in ownership that delivers value.

I know building and delivering intellectual equity might sound like a tough discovery process.

Go Patel

Neil Patel is a personal branding superstar. His agency, NP Digital, is a leading digital marketing agency that specializes in SEO, content, social, and paid media. NP's client base includes SoFi, Adobe, LinkedIn, Direct TV, and Ricoh.

INTELLECTUAL PROPERTY

Adweek named NP Digital the sixth-fastest growing agency in 2021. The agency increased its revenues by 585% from 2018 to 2020 by diversifying.

How did NP Digital jump ahead of the digital pack? It's all about audience interest, baby. Some numbers based on Neil's delivery of daily digital marketing information and advice, and superior personal branding:

- 9 million visits to the Neil Patel blog every month
- Over 1 million YouTube subscribers—over 1 million views per month
- 1 million monthly downloads of Neil's daily Marketing School podcast. I listen to it every morning.

But wait. There's more.

NP Digital builds and buys intellectual equity. They built the SEO SaaS tool Ubersuggest.

Ubersuggest offers keyword suggestions, content ideas, competitor analysis and backlink data. It generates over 3 million users per month and is priced 90% less than competitive tools from Moz, Ahrefs, and SEMrush that charge $950 to $9,900 a year. Better yet, it does double duty—it drives IP-driven revenues *and* incoming leads to the agency.

I'm not suggesting that you spend the time, energy, and big bucks to build an Ubersuggest or Basecamp SaaS solution. However, I am suggesting that you look at what type of intellectual equity you could deliver.

Go White Label

White labeling is when another company does the heavy lifting (idea gen + programming + design), and you get to brand its service as your own.

Some Resources

AppSumo lists over 30 tech programs that can be white labeled. Programs include video editing services, project management systems, and even social media tools. One example is Rumble Studio, which can help make your agency stand out in the world of podcast production:

> Rumble Studio is an audio recording solution that lets you conduct remote interviews and produce content quickly.

Social media tracking tool Awario can be white labeled.
Big boy Ogilvy white labels the client and agency reporting tool Funnel.
But wait, there's more: Take a page out of the 37signals Basecamp book and dial it up... Y'all can take the art and science of digital skill sets one mega step further.
The Colorado advertising agency Huebner Integrated Marketing was such a nimble developer that it built the company White Label IQ, a sister agency that creates white-labeled SaaS and PPC services for other agencies. Here's a nice message from the White label IQ website:

> We understand the cadence and digital skillsets clients demand through our origins from a marketing agency. As a result, our partnerships with other agencies provide design, Development, SaaS and PPC capacity with specialized skill sets that make agency life easier and more profitable.

Your agency has multiple white label paths. If you build it, they will come. If you white label it from another party, they will come. If you build it, you can sell it as a SaaS service to another agency.

Productizing the Agency

Productizing your services involves packaging, delivering, and selling your services as if they were a tangible product.
Two product(ized) ideas.

The Service Product—Brand Your Secret Sauce

Clients look for a creative agency that has a proven management and production system that is focused on their needs.

For example, leverage a client pain point and build out your branded solution.

One certain pain point is a client's fear that an agency doesn't listen hard enough. It might not get to the client's real needs and goals versus what the agency wants to deliver. So, prove your listenership skill set with a branded system.

Example: Create and brand a productized new client onboarding system with scheduled six-month "How are we doing?" reviews—a system that demonstrates and sells in how you work to meet client objectives.

Agencies often have systems for initial discovery, research, and ideation. Consider packaging and branding them.

You could also take a discrete program, create your very own system, and productize it. Don't take my word for it. From Jake Jorgovan of Content Allies, a company that builds branded revenue-generating podcasts:

> The biggest benefit of a productized service is that you sell the exact same thing every time. There is no customization, no proposals, and no back and forth. You have a conversation, evaluate if it is a fit, and then they either buy or don't buy.

Make the scope very clear. Define it. Brand it. Price it.

Go Small

A blue-sky example… build XYZ Agency's Blog-o-Rama. For $9,000 the client gets a blog post strategy, creative brief, SEO guidance document, process and calendar doc, and three starter blog posts.

Too small for you?

CHAPTER 8

This might sound like a small-agency product, but I think larger agencies could use this idea, or a related idea, as a "Get to know us" program that offers the client a taste of your magic and customer service that will lead to more business. Clearly your mileage may vary. However, making an initial purchase of an agency system easy for a client is a good thing.

In this case, your product acts like a paid amuse-bouche.

Wait, Wait

A productization idea...

The branding company Designjoy offers design as a subscription. A design product. Billing starts at $4,995/m.

This one-man shop has reported annual recurring revenues of over $1.5 million. From Brett Williams's LinkedIn profile:

Designjoy a one-person premium design service currently serving 40+ clients with a $1.5M ARR.

On his website:

A design agency with a twist.

Apps, websites, logos & more.

From his FAQ: Why wouldn't I just hire a full-time designer?

Good question! For starters, the annual cost of a full-time senior-level designer now exceeds $100,000, plus benefits (and good luck finding one available). Aside from that, you may not always have enough work to keep them busy at all times, so you're stuck paying for time you aren't able to utilize.

With the monthly plan, you can pause and resume your subscription as often as you need to ensure you're only paying your designer when you have work available for them.

INTELLECTUAL PROPERTY

Brett's solo Instagram has over 74K Followers. 35K Followers on Twitter. The mega agency VMLY&R has 57K followers and, get this, 16K employees.

Now the very serious stuff. From a 2023 Tweet at @designjoy:

Just started tracking my spending habits and budgeting. Designjoy now costs less than $400/m to run. That's it. That's my overhead. And half of that is a Shutterstock subscription. Agencies are doing it all wrong.

Wait. Wait. There's more. You can now dive into Brett's *Productize Yourself* course for $99. Of course, you should sign up for his *productized* course.

Has your agency ever considered running a series of courses?

CHAPTER 9

CHAPTER 9
24/7 Business Development

Stop with the Shoemaker Excuse

It has been reported that most advertising agencies don't have a comprehensive business development plan. Yes, this sounds like Chapter 2's missing business plan.

A yikes coming... Most of the agencies with a business development plan do not consistently run the plan they designed.

I hear a lot of excuses from large, medium, and small advertising agencies about why they aren't running a long-term, 24/7 business development program. These agencies often chuckle—a wary chuckle—before mentioning the infamous cobbler's shoe excuse.

You know what I'm talking about. The excuse is that the agency is so focused on its day-to-day clients that it neglects its own business development—or better expressed, their own sales program. These agencies act like the way-too-busy shoemaker whose children go barefoot: "Yup, I'm like really busy making shoes for my customers. Just don't have the time to take care of the kids."

Of course, this is insanity. Some agencies enter a serious failure zone because one of their large, cash-cow clients leaves and the agency doesn't have a prospect pipeline that will deliver the next big account. My mantra is that we all know clients will walk out the back door and you must have new ones to come in the front. Keep the pipeline full. A duh? Yes.

Building the Plan

There are a billion experts, websites, blogs, books, white papers, podcasts, and videos that discuss how to build out a business development plan—a sales plan. I'm going to hit the most important elements.

Good news: Just like the one-page business plan, business development plans do not have to be biblical.

The Core Elements of a Power Plan

1. **Position your agency for growth.**
   Be an expert. B2B buyers want experts who understand their business, their category, and their issues and opportunities.

2. **Act different.**
   Not all expert positions are truly different. However, do what you do for your clients and craft and enunciate the positioning, so it stands out. As Apple once said, "Think different."

3. **Set goals.**
   These can be defined as SMART goals: Specific, Measurable, Achievable, Relevant, and Time Bound. Have KPI objectives and know how to assess.

4. **Define your target market.**
   Categories, companies, job titles (à la CMO and CFO), and real people (get beyond titles). Consider building personas for the people and groups you need to excite.

5. **Determine your best marketing channels.**
   Selection should be based on what inbound and outbound B2B channels work in your space and what you can get done ("Keep it simple, stupid!").

6. **Be unignorable.**
   Back to thinking different... and looking different too. Once a year I head to YouTube for the TBWA/Chiat/Day Apple "Here's to the Crazy Ones" and the 1984 Macintosh launch commercials. Pure inspiration. While you are at it, watch Steve Job's iPhone introduction.

7. **Be consistent.**
   Be 24/7, baby. You never know when that next great client will be searching for you. Use a production calendar.

8. **Develop a process.**
   Create and run a well-defined process and system to manage the work.

9. **Manage agency resources.**
   Business development is stressful. Manage resources to avoid staff burnout.

10. **Systemize client "selection."**
    Have a system to determine what requests for information (RFIs), requests for proposals (RFPs), and pitch invitations you should respond to—and importantly, should not respond to.

Given burnout awareness, I'm seeing many agencies back off from the never-ending pitch cycle. Use my Go-No-Go Pitch Quiz that's in the Resources section.

A Deep-Dive Assessment

I always start my client engagements with two tools to help assess an agency's goals, strengths, and weaknesses.

My agency business development questionnaire is designed to be a starting point—a way for me to begin to dig into the agency, its history, objectives, and so on.

Second, an agency SWOT (strengths, weaknesses, opportunities, and threats) analysis is designed to ascertain what's working and what's not.

The Levitan Business Development Questionnaire

This is how I onboard my new agency clients:

> I have a few general questions to help us kick off. Your brief (or detailed) responses will help me to get to know your agency's objectives, market position, and strategies so I can begin to formulate a set of opinions and recommendations to help you grow your agency.
>
> *Questions*
> Do you have a master agency business plan? If so, when was the last time you revised it?
>
> Do you have an active business development plan?
>
> If you do, what is and isn't working?

Who at your company is most responsible for business development? Is business development currently an agency-wide effort?

What is your agency's core brand positioning or sales proposition? Do you have a focused elevator pitch?

Is your current brand position competitive—do you think it stands out from the pack?

What have been the key reasons clients have hired you?

Do you specialize today or want to in the future (in, e.g., a business category, media, technology)?

Do you have a geographic concentration—local, regional, national, or global?

Do you have any unique, standout intellectual properties or marketing solutions?

Can you describe what a cherished high-value client looks like?

What are the top five new clients you would like to add to your roster? Note: Clients you think would choose you. Why would they do this?

Do you currently have a strong client-lead pipeline?

How have you been getting your best new client leads?

What percentage of new leads are the result of referrals or word of mouth?

Do you participate I head-to-head pitch presentations or are clients just asking for proposals?

Do you have a standardized RFI or RFP format?

What do you view as your biggest business issues (your positioning, missing skill sets, business development, geography, staff, etc.)?

What other factors inhibit growth? Competitive agencies, new business models, client inertia, macroeconomic issues, etc.?

What agencies are your direct competitors?

Are there any agencies or marketing companies in general that impress you? Why?

Agency resources: If I suggest a thought leadership program (social media, cases, research, white papers, videos, etc.) do you have the internal resources or partners that can help get the work done?

What's your end game? You don't need to have one today. However, some agency owners or leaders have a desire to build a sellable agency. Knowing this helps to focus on a value-building path.

A SWOT Analysis

I also ask my clients to do a SWOT analysis. An agency SWOT analysis provides a top-level perspective on an agency's opportunities and issues. Strengths and weaknesses represent current conditions; threats and opportunities represent the future.

Consider having multiple people do a SWOT on their own. Is the leadership team on the same page? You might be surprised at the often-disparate results.

CHAPTER 10
The Optimal Agency Website

Always Revising

Ta da! Here's to yet another new agency website.

Virtually every advertising agency I talk with is considering revising or rebuilding their website. Some even days after launching a new one since it took the agency seven months to build the latest site and it's now looking stale to your designers. You know what I'm talking about.

This recurring need for new comes with the marketing services landscape. We are on the frontlines of both design and evolving technology. We design stuff for a living so our designy UI and UX stuff better look and sound good.

We want to believe our website is so compelling and informative and convincing that visitors will stay awhile and learn all about us. And make one-on-one contact.

Not so fast.

CHAPTER 10

The sales guru Daniel Pink reminds us that we've moved from *caveat emptor*, the Latin maxim that means "let the buyer beware," to *caveat venditor*, meaning "let the seller beware." This is because a client will most likely examine your agency and its sales proposition before you ever know they looked at you. In fact, you may never know they stopped by in the first place—or how long they stayed.

Generalizations First

Gartner's corporate executive board reported that B2B buyers are 57% of the way to a buying decision before they're willing to talk to a sales rep. *Caveat venditor.*

An agency website is, at first, a B2B sales tool. It should strive to entice a visitor to let you know that they visited. It is a mega wasted effort if they like the look and feel of your website but are not enticed to make contact.

Website Musts

Be clear about who you are and what you offer. Get to the point.

Build the website to meet visitor needs, not to make your strategy and creative teams feel good.

Use clear navigation.

Have some personality. People buy people. Friendly is good.

It is OK to want to be cool but strive to initiate contact. Make a visitor an offer they can't refuse.

The 10-Second Website Rule

The bottom line: Prospective clients give an agency website mere seconds to introduce the agency and learn about what it can do for them.

People, all people, exhibit some form of attention deficit disorder. We know this as marketers. To gain several minutes of user attention, you must clearly communicate your value proposition within 10 seconds.

Ten seconds. How did I get to this number?

I used the research of the UX/UI expert Jacob Nielsen as reported by the NN/g Nielsen Norman Group. According to Nielsen, 10 seconds is what you get.

> It's clear that the first 10 seconds of the page visit are critical for users' decision to stay or leave. The probability of leaving is very high during these first few seconds because users are extremely skeptical, having suffered countless poorly designed web pages in the past.
>
> If the web page survives this first—extremely harsh—10-second judgment, users will look around a bit. However, they're still highly likely to leave during the subsequent 20 seconds of their visit. Only after people have stayed on a page for about 30 seconds does the curve become relatively flat.

A quick question: Did you use any of this 10-second fast-in and fast-out thinking to build your agency's website?

OK, don't come after me. If your website was designed by a design-first creative director without a solid sales-oriented creative brief that recognized what I'll call WDD, website deficit disorder, then, um, some seriously high home page bounce rates will happen.

Three Optimized Elements

Once hooked, a prospective client will look hard at the agency website for a clear understanding of what you can do for them via your sales proposition (the sales pitch), clients you have worked for (proof), past work and cases (proof), awards (third-party support), agency thought leadership, and, importantly in a world of agency sameness, agency personality. And these days, for an increasing number of clients, your agency culture.

Stating the obvious... your website is a critical sales tool. You know this. However, my years of building websites (my first was for Microsoft in 1998) and deconstructing hundreds of agency websites demonstrates that many are not following Nielsen's 10-second rule.

Here are my three rules for having an attention-grabbing website.

1. KISS: Keep it simple, stupid!

You have that 10-second window to capture the attention and interest of a visitor to begin to sell them. I am a fan of simple, fast-read design.

Simple (and fast) is good.

Once upon a time, M&C Saatchi told prospects what they will get from the agency as soon as the visitor hit the home page.

In large type the agency delivered their very direct sales pitch. Their USP:

> BRUTAL SIMPLICITY OF THOUGHT.
> It is easier to complicate than simplify.
> Simple ideas enter the brain quicker and stay there longer.
> Brutal simplicity of thought is therefore a painful necessity.

Maurice called the delivery of this simplicity message one-word equity. At that time, the agency sold the idea of simplicity—can you imagine them having a complex design to express this thought?

This direct statement of keeping it simple works in today's overstimulated website deficit disorder world. "Hope" helped define the Obama brand.

A look at even more simple. This time it's simple served up with humor.

NYC Walrus agency's website stars a talking walrus (how's that for branding?). You input a question and the walrus delivers an answer.

In case you think it's all left up to the talking walrus, the home page also includes a drop-down menu of the usual navigation (Home, Work, Info, News). They also point to the agency's Facebook, Instagram, Twitter, and Medium pages.

While Walrus might seem to break my Rule 2 (see below), they deliver on their advertising philosophy and distinctive message—humor works—which seems to attract their nice client list and sweet awards.

Even more simple.

The digital and experiential agency Puppy Love opens with their giving a visitor the opportunity to choose a voice (cowboy, ASMR, or Aunt Ruthie) and a background color that delivers the agency's sale proposition. The voice and color thing is both simple and different. I chose a cowboy and lavender and got this message in cowboy speak:

WE BUILD DIGITAL AND PHYSICAL EXPERIENCES FOR BRANDS WHO WANT TO BE DIFFERENT.

Why the interactive voice and color action? Well, it does deliver on and supports the "being different experience" message and, hey, why not be interactive to grab the attention of that WDD (website deficit disorder) visitor? It also quickly ups the interactive time spent on the home page.

2. Salesmanship rocks.

The agency website must sell. It is its reason for being. You have those measly 10 seconds to say something that grabs and then drives the visitor to your sales pitch.

Look at your competition and ask if they deliver an action-oriented, sales-oriented message. Probably not. Too many agencies fear "selling."

M&C Saatchi quickly sold the idea of simplicity. Walrus quickly sells the idea that advertising can be fun. Both work because M&C Saatchi is a recognized brand and Walrus's talking walrus is hard to ignore and delivers the message that these guys are funny—and goes further to sell.

On the day I'm writing this book, Walrus has an offer on their front page. They're asking advertisers if they have their Super Bowl spot. If Walrus's spot isn't ranked in the top five, the client doesn't have to pay for production. This offer got the attention of Ad Age. I am sure the agency will always sell-in their being "different." Simple "different." Fun "different."

Go direct marketing.

Portland's The Good is an ecommerce conversion rate specialist. Its site is designed to sell via The Good's very focused pitch that immediately nails a big client pain point:

> 98% of your website visitors won't buy from you today.
> We improve your conversion rate turning more visitors into buyers.

The Good's website puts a client pain point front and center (poor conversion). It's followed by "We can help…" (a "call us" message) and clear navigation to action.

The home page also includes proof, as in conversion and revenue increases for clients, including Xerox at 86.7%, Easton at 240%, and Swiss Gear at 132%. Plus, and I really dig this approach, they have a one-minute video that tells their data-backed science story to deliver a sales pitch.

They also offer two agency principle books. More proof that they are a CRO expert and thought leader.

The agency's results and cases are also direct and clear. Each case funnels to a contact form.

3. Personality, please.

Every website has a distinct personality. Walrus is smart fun. The Good is a conversion specialist that walks its talk.

Too many agency websites just provide lists. Our mission, our services, our work, our clients, our people, our locations. Too often these factoids are delivered without any personality. Your personality just might be your differentiator.

More thoughts on personality to come. But first, someone please steal this stand-up comedy idea…

Once upon a time I thought that it would be "different" to have my agency's website open with a video of a stand-up comedian riffing on the advertising industry and our wonderful agency. "Take my agency… please." (By the way, that line riffs on the comedian Henny Youngman's "Take my wife… please." Under 45? Check him out on YouTube.)

Why would I consider using a comedian to introduce the agency? I am a believer in the power of humor to arrest attention. Plus, this angle gives the agency a personality in a generally personality-free zone. And I guarantee a comedian will keep a visitor on the home page for longer than 10 seconds.

Yeah, I have an opinion. However, I'm not alone. From the *Harvard Business Review*:

> The workplace needs laughter. According to research from institutions as serious as Wharton, MIT, and London Business School, every chuckle or guffaw brings with it a host of business benefits. Laughter relieves stress and boredom, boosts engagement and well-being, and spurs not only creativity and collaboration but also analytic precision and productivity.

Go ahead and take this humor-first idea… please.

A unique example of leading with humor is the creative and production studio ADWEAK. The agency drives interest—for example, its 100,000 Twitter followers—via its unique look at agency and client life.

- BREAKING: Agency Just Listing Anything They Can Think of on Capabilities Slide for New Business Pitch
- BREAKING: Agency Staffers Still Have No Idea what Recently

CHAPTER 10

> Hired "Thought Leader" Actually Does
> - BREAKING: Client Plans to Wait Until After She Receives Holiday Gift from Agency Before Announcing Review
> - BREAKING: VLMY&R Considers Adding Another Couple Letters to Name

The ADWEAK website has few words but delivers this compelling key message:

We're good, we're smart, we're fast and we're not A-holes.

Try some humor if you've got it in you, please.

Website Navigation

If you have only 10 seconds to grab interest for your sales pitch, better do it fast. Challenge yourself by asking, Why should a prospect pay attention? Or worse, Why wouldn't they just click away?

The Home Page

There is no one size fits all. However, your home page must do a couple of things right.

Branding
Your primary objective is to deliver a branded sales proposition. The sales pitch doesn't have to be hardcore—just not normcore.

Do a competitive check of your competition to make sure that you look and sound different. I'd like to think this does happen. But a perusal of 10 kinda-look-alike agency websites will indicate that this is not standard practice.

Nudge a Bit

Activate the power of *nudge*.

The world of behavioral economics includes the concept of creating a nudge. This idea comes from the book *Nudge: The Final Edition*, written by Nobel Prize–winning Richard Thaler and Cass A. Sunstein.

They postulate that

> A choice architect has the responsibility for organizing the context in which people make decisions.
>
> A nudge, as we will use the term, is any aspect of the choice architecture that alters people's behavior in a predictable way without forbidding any options or significantly changing their economic incentives.

Bottom line: You are a communicator whose clients pay to generate an action. What action do *you* want *your* website visitor to take, and how will you nudge them along?

Navigation Elements

Most agencies have similar navigation elements. Here is my quick take on how to deliver clout in each of the most used website sections.

OK. But. Your agency might not need all these elements. One way to assess this decision is if you think that you have a seriously hot shit and to the point sales proposition or irresistible offer that would make the visitor that come-on that they can't refuse. Another is that you subscribe to the less-is-more school of communications.

Adweak Studio's website is an example of brevity. They sell their own brand of creative via a home page with a humorous sizzle reel and a 113 word About page. That's all folks. Of course, it helps that their 100K Twitter follower account delivers an average of over 3 million Twitter impressions a month.

On to more.

CHAPTER 10

About. And About Us

There are many routes to delivering the About message. These include your mission, agency story, and services.

Here's how three of Ad Age's Small Agency winners describe themselves.

Movers+Shakers delivers a clear sales proposition (as in what's in it for clients):

> CONNECTING BRANDS TO CULTURE.
>
> Movers+Shakers is a disruptive creative agency on a mission to spread joy. By connecting brands to culture, we drive brand love.
>
> Our clients rely on us to push them into tomorrow, creating cultural relevance across mainstream and emerging social platforms.

Fitzco delivers the agency's internal culture message:

> We're an independent and integrated team that thrives in the trenches together. When you see how our media, strategy, and creative work effortlessly and quickly together, you'll understand that we're united in a simple principle. The collaboration, the work, the results, our people, our culture—it all matters to us.
>
> Our agency's mission is pretty simple: to care deeply, learn continuously and push creatively to deliver business solutions that have a real-world impact.

Alto starts out really good. I like the home page message as it defines the clients they want:

> A creative company for courageous brands.

Inside Alto gets a bit too me-too:

> We are a creative company that is structured to make industry-changing work and partner exactly in the way our clients require: Centered around a lean core of highly experienced players, our team is scaled to fit the needs of each client and project.

Isn't this every agency?

Your agency's About page is a significant chance to make sure that visiting future clients will like you. It's an opportunity to shine.

Act different.

Our People

People buy people. In many business development pitches, the decision comes down to which agency people the decision-maker team likes more. Given the similarities between agencies, especially pitch finalists that have similar expertise stories, the people factor matters. Simpatico is a good thing.

This people thing applies to agency websites. How you show your people matters. It matters to prospective clients but also, and importantly, to your current *and* future staff. Future employees want to work with people who look and sound cool, smart, caring and experienced.

Some Our People musts to think through:

1. Decide how many and which people to show. If it's a small agency, you could show everyone. Does this make you look too small? These days small is good. Large agencies must prune the list. Just management? Is this too hierarchical?
2. Determine your look. Do the portraits have similar attributes? Are they high quality? Similar lighting and background? I like it when agencies have a look that makes everyone appear like they work at the same place. Of course, this goal gets strained due to remote work. Try on some Photoshop.

3. Should you consider using video vs. static photos? More video haranguing coming later.
4. How much description to add is a big decision. Just a title? Roles, experience, achievements?
5. Should you link to people's social media profiles? Linking to a LinkedIn profile would allow a visitor to dig in deeper. However, you'd better trust your people to keep their profiles up to date and professional.
6. How can you humanize your staff? You could just have a photograph and a name. Or you could inject some personality.

These agencies Our People pages are worth a look:

Digital Marmalade's Meet the Team page uses some interactivity. Play with the images.

Zulu Alpha Kilo, not surprising, uses humor on its Crew page. Watch the video. Please. And, yes, what a unique idea—video to introduce agency human beings.

Creative Theory combines photos with animation, unique copy ("Ashlee Green is an agitator of potential" rather than just her business title—"Sr. Account Manager"), and each bio includes the employee's email. A nice personal touch.

The humorous Wexley School for Girls (a now long-lost agency) used photos of models—not the real folks. Who doesn't want to work with attractive people? The Wexley list was not ignorable and helped to drive home their unique attitude.

Our Work
Of course, the Our Work section is all about "show me the money." Clients want to see standout creative work, ideas, and strategies (often media strategies) that sell.

The Our Work section tells the visitor the clients you've worked with and the breadth of your communications skills. And, of course, that you are a creative thinker that delivers a high degree of power thinking and action.

On to the multiclient sizzle reel. Sizzle reels work some of the time. In my take, most are kinda run-on video sentences with little explanation or reason to pay attention. I think the reel could work harder if you lead the viewer through the work. Consider adding some text to both inform and excite. Too many sizzle reels deliver visual headaches that leave way too much understanding to the viewer. Adweak Studio's sizzle is actually about their delivery of sizzle.

Our Cases
Cases sell. Sell big time.

State the objective, then the work (or thinking), and then offer some results. Keep it simple and fast. Be strategic in your approach.

LONDON Advertising once upon a time went beyond just showing case histories to having a unique branded way—an ownable way—to frame their cases via the ownable term "straight-line thinking." From objective to delivery to success. In all cases, the agency supported their main message: They create one single marketing idea that can work around the world.

Here's an example of straight-line thinking for the Mandarin Oriental Hotel Group client.

The case leads with a print ad: a portrait of the actor Morgan Freeman and the line "He's a fan."

Product: Fantastic hotels.

Strategy: The rich and famous choose to stay there.

One Brilliant Idea: "He's a fan."

The Outcome: Group has grown 500% since campaign launch.

I don't need paragraphs of case copy to understand the direct communication of this explicit approach.

Why not use your agency's very own business development case study? Did you employ a brilliant strategy for your own sales? Show how you used out-of-the-box inbound marketing. Podcasting. LinkedIn, Short videos, landing pages. Walk your talk. Preen a bit. It is also a way for you to sell in the idea of a different marketing approach. If you do it for you, you can do it for the client.

Our Services
Sure, talk about your services. Just consider that long lists of services that range from strategy to digital prowess to TV commercial production to influencer marketing to experiential to PR to UX mastery are not particularly convincing.

I'll use the analogy of the 10-page New Jersey diner menu. In this case the menu from New Jersey's Mark Twain Diner. How can this one-location diner make omelets, BBQ pulled-pork nachos, fried calamari, Philly cheese steak sandwiches, baked Greek spinach pie, pierogis, Maryland crab cake salad, avocado toast, quesadillas, bistec encebollado, coconut-crusted chicken salad, Cuban paninis, Jack Daniel's smokehouse full rack of ribs, and of course grilled cheese? In one kitchen. OK, I will stop. You get the idea.

I know why some of you want long lists of services. But there has to be a better way to present your integrated skills than with a run-on and run-on diner-menu approach.

Can you condense your list into a singular client-benefit story or wrap it into a branded service product? Give your list a reason for being. Relate the list back to your master brand.

Testimonials
I love third-party proof. Testimonials deliver proof. These can be copy or video based (entertaining and brief videos, please.)

Be different. What if you had a short video channel just for testimonials?

One ad agency had their current clients telling website visitors that they would never leave their agency despite getting sales pitches from competitive agencies every week. It was an interesting way to sell-in the value of the agency. An agency that was irresistible.

Our Clients

Clients like to see a *list*. Who have you worked with? Are you desirable? Client history is proof. Client lists are delivered via names, logos and the work itself.

That said, what should make up your list? Keep in mind that the future client might go beyond the logos to ask for details.

Do you just show the work the agency did? Do you include past clients? Like, you did a one-off project for AT&T in 2018. How far back do you think you could go?

Do you include the mention of clients your staff might have worked on at other agencies? Here are two examples as food for thought.

My Oregon agency specialized in health-care clients. Of course, we listed the agency's very own current and past health-care clients. But what about my own multiyear health-care client history that preceded my Oregon tenure? I had worked with Johnson & Johnson around the world. Did I include J&J in our client history? You bet. Hey, any new client would have gotten my experience, so why not state it?

Your agency is made up of people who have past business experience. Why not say that your ECD worked on Hilton? On the other hand, do you list Honda if your only touch was that your junior copywriter had once done some Honda CRV banner ads at Hakuhodo? Um, no.

Brains. Blogs, Podcasts, Etc.

Industry research studies indicate that clients want strategic thinking based on an agency's experience and foresight.

I like stating the obvious. So be a showoff.

I'm going to call this website section "brains". This is where you show your brainiac thinking. Agencies call this section different names:
- Blog
- Strategic Insights
- Thought Leadership
- Ideas
- Opinions

- Journal

Whatever you call this section. It needs to meet at least these three objectives:
1. The agency must sound smart and have a unique and competitive perspective. I see way too many me-too blog posts that will get lost in the wind. In most cases, Google doesn't care what you've written if it mirrors the agency down the block.
2. The agency must deliver insights that immediately relate to its prospect's information needs and, yup, those pesky pain points. This is the opportunity to look like the leader that will propel the client forward.
3. The agency needs to leverage the art and science of search engine optimization when choosing what to write about. Write for your audience, but don't forget about what Google cherishes.

Brains is where an agency can go big. I've included ideas in Chapter 6, "Thought Leadership."

A plus: The agency's brains section demonstrates that the agency can do social media marketing for itself. A savvy client will notice that you get SEM and SEO from reading your headlines and action-oriented thinking.

Be very efficient. Once you have that blog post or podcast interview or white paper, amplify it across other platforms.

Our Culture

Clients, employees, and, importantly, prospective employees are now looking hard at agency culture. Agency values, beliefs, and your mission matter.

From Havas Canada's "People and Culture" page:

> Diversity and inclusion. We believe great businesses are built on great cultures. We are taking tangible steps to create a genuinely

inclusive culture within our Villages. That means providing opportunity for all of our people to succeed.

Dallas's Hawkeye says:

> People are at the heart of everything we do. Ours is a culture without ego. But full of ambition—a place that celebrates diversity, empowers creativity, and accelerates careers.

One could say these are just words. But, today, words like these need to be said—and backed up. People can sniff out BS.

Speaking of getting past BS and pablum, go look at Mojo Supermarket's 2022 World Cup series "The Slavery Cup" on Agency Spy. Mojo put their agency culture on the street via projections on FIFA and UN office buildings.

Go Fact Sheet

Most websites are information rich. So much so that most of us can't remember all of what we read, watched, and loved. Understatement: The website visit can be ephemeral, as in a fleeting memory.

Help your prospects remember you by giving them facts and info to download and hold in their hands. It can be a one-sheet PDF that can easily be shared within a client organization.

Deliver all the information in one place that an attention deficit marketing director needs.

Please Ask for Contact

Driving contact is where the rubber meets the road. A tour of agency websites shows a wide range of contact pages. Most are too weak. Some (most) just provide an email contact. Some contact pages go for it by providing reasons to make contact. These contact pages are much more assertive than just having a passive contact email form.

I am a strong believer that the contact section should be warm and welcoming. Businesslike but friendly. Contact should be an invitation and a metaphorical fist bump.

Bland does not work for me. I need some online hospitality. This is a place to show some personality. Even humor. Even empathy. Try to get past the passive voice. Ask for the order. Gently. Not too Glengarry Glenn Ross.

Instead of bland text, why not deliver a 20-second video on why we should talk?

Given people's general inertia, go ahead and tell the visitor to make contact. Consider how to give them a good reason to act. Maybe make an offer to capture attention and a reaction. This isn't a brand-new idea—SaaS companies do this all the time because it works.

Here is what I say on my Contact page:

Three reasons to contact me.
1. I deliver the most creative approach to advertising agency positioning and lead generation.
2. I am the most experienced agency business development coach. Read the "My Story" page. I stole the idea from Austin Kleon.
3. My goal is to make your advertising agency unignorable. Unignorable drives awareness and action. Think of the alternative.

I deliver an offer...

Take me up on my free Corleone Godfather offer.

This is an offer you can't—or rather, shouldn't—refuse.

Let's talk for thirty minutes—just 0.50 on the timesheet—to discuss your agency's issues and opportunities and how I will help you build a more powerful advertising agency business development plan.

Does my Godfather offer work? Yes.

Does my Gandhi testimonial video at the bottom of the page help? Yes.

Chicago's Orbit Media website development firm goes a bit further than most agencies. They address the fact that the client might just be ready for them. They have this interactive dialogue-building offer on the Contact page:

> Have a project but not quite ready to contact us? See if Orbit is a fit for you.

Last point. Do not ask for too much information. You do not need the prospect's date of birth.

Video, Please

Too few agencies include brand-building video on their website. If they do, there's a high degree of chance that it will be a sizzle reel.

I prefer a video that helps deliver the agency's USP. The digital agency HawkSEM opens with an animated video that clearly states the agency's mantra and client benefits—in 10 seconds:

> We could start by talking and bragging about award this and featuring that, but who cares? We believe in results. At the end of the day delivering measurable marketing results, predictable revenue, and high ROI is what matters.

Another approach is to put a real human in the video. Why not have an agency leader deliver the message, and while they're at it, also deliver some agency soul? You can make a compelling video introduction. You are creative.

Videos engage, are more memorable, and are better at brand recall than text and... increase buying intent.

Still with me? MarketingProfs reports that "the average user spends

88% more time on a website with video than a website without one." How can one ignore this 88% finding?

The Power of Landing Pages

Landing pages, short form micro-websites that hammer a single point and encourage a visitor to act now, should be considered if you target specific client categories and want to hype a singular agency expertise.

Example one: I worked with a media planning and buying agency that created a separate micro site for their white label planning services for third-party agencies. They did not want to confuse their marketing clients by having them see the two services aimed at two different audiences.

Example two: Another agency wanted to point to their financial prowess but did not want to confuse their more universal UX/UI design clients. They hyped their financial services on a landing page promoted via direct to category ABM marketing.

Landing pages, due to their simplicity and direct relationship to an inbound or outbound sales message and often offer, can dramatically increase conversion rates. Many leading SaaS companies use landing pages to drive interest and immediate action. They make their visitor a fast, concise offer they can't refuse.

Check out landing page best practices at Unbounce and HubSpot.

CHAPTER 11
Inbound or Outbound Marketing?

Oh My. In. Out. What to Do?

When I was asked to run business development at Saatchi & Saatchi, I called up Jonathan Bond of New York's very successful Kirshenbaum & Bond (now KBS) and asked him what business development strategies worked best for his successful agency. He said they were not exactly sure what were the hardest-working tactics, so they did everything. Admittedly this was back before data took over the universe to tell us exactly what works. Um, wow, that is wishful thinking.

I mention this conversation because even today with reams of conversion data, there isn't a one-size-fits-all approach to building the perfect business development program. Advertising, PR, ecommerce, SEM, email, strategic, branding, experiential (I'll save you from my going on and on) agencies and their unique expertise and prospective clients are way too different for a one-size-fits-all program.

This gets me to the often-asked agency question: What is more efficient and effective, inbound or outbound marketing?

Let's start with definitions.

Inbound Marketing = Attraction

From HubSpot:

> Inbound marketing is a business methodology that attracts customers by creating valuable content and experiences tailored to them.

From Marketo:

> Inbound marketing is the process of helping potential customers find your company.

From me:
> Inbound marketing is an always-on content-based strategy that responds to demonstrated buyer intent.

My first foray into inbound marketing was in the mid-1990s when I was CEO of the award-winning New Jersey Online, a very early online newspaper with more traffic than the online New York Times. One of our most potent traffic drivers was our online forum section (a community bulletin board). Our forum's communities offered discussion zones for New York and New Jersey's eight professional sports teams and state-wide youth sports.

When kids and parents discussed their Saturday games, other parents and kids chimed in. The forums were a very compelling, very attractive 24/7 community magnet. Forums delivered inbound attraction. Forums were the early edge of our world of social media.

Today's inbound marketing activity, the art and science of getting the right people to find your company, spans SEO, PPC, must-read content, new social media, and audio and video broadcast platforms. Unfortunately, driving inbound interest via the Google business model is getting harder and harder.

It's getting Harder

Once upon a time it was a Google search world that thrived on SEO. Today a client looking for an agency might, stress might, use Google. Even using Google search, it is freaking difficult to get on page one or even three.

These days prospects could be searching for you on Instagram, LinkedIn, YouTube, TikTok, Dribble, Behance, on award websites, and use word of mouth care of your active referral program.

Plus, AI search will become (is) a serious search platform.

Outbound Marketing = Direct Marketing

I had a good laugh a few years ago care of one of my adverting agency clients. The agency's Dubai-based CEO had spent much of his career at Microsoft, and his marketing lingo included the first time I had ever heard the term account-based marketing. I asked for a definition. He described direct marketing and its century-old strategy and tactics. I laughed.

Account-based marketing (ABM) is outbound direct marketing.

Two Expert Definitions

From Marketo:

> Account-based marketing—or key account marketing—uses the

combined expertise of the marketing and sales teams to target select groups of accounts that require tailored marketing.

From Gartner:

> Account-based marketing (ABM) is a go-to-market strategy targeting certain accounts with a synchronized, continuous set of marketing and sales activities. ABM activities engage those accounts and individuals through all stages of the buying journey.
>
> Key descriptors being key account marketing; select groups of accounts; synchronized, continuous set of activities.

While some marketing gurus prefer SEM-generated inbound to outbound, I prefer a combination. Because doing both can be highly efficient if you combine and repurpose your efforts.

Do Both? But...

I think that in today's cluttered business development information universe outbound, as in ABM, works harder than inbound. Harder? ABM provides the platform and systems that leverage your expert positioning to go after the specific clients and categories that deserve your brains.

Today's inbound effectiveness is constrained by the massive amount of content of all types and the fact that managing SEO itself has gotten more difficult. An example of content overload: I just counted that I have 25 advertising- and marketing-oriented podcasts listed in my podcast app. Twenty-five!

A Google search on "healthcare SEO agency" yields 3,510 results with seven ads and eight listings on Google's first page. What are your odds for getting a free listing on this page?

However, inbound still needs to be in your marketing mix. You just need to be more strategic and meld and execute the art and science of content marketing. So, no, you are not getting an inbound pass. With smart workload planning you can do it all—well, the smart stuff.

CHAPTER 12

CHAPTER 12

Account-Based Marketing

Four Mantras

In this section, I cover a range of ABM tactics. As mentioned earlier, there is overlap between outbound and inbound marketing. All content can be sliced and diced and delivered to meet tactical objectives.

There are four mantras of ABM:

1. Directly meet the current and future information needs of your market. Do the required market research to find those hot buttons. I like future think because we are all looking over the horizon for how to deal with the disruption that is for sure coming next.
2. Market to a well-researched and well-designed prospect list. Building the right list is critical. It allows your impressive thought leadership to be delivered directly to your key prospects through persona development, personalization, and optimized reach and

frequency.
3. Have agency methodology to help edit and build out the thought leadership program. Consider using the ICE scoring model, which can assign numerical values to ideas. Prioritize them via an assessment of impact, confidence, and ease.
4. Keep it simple, stupid! There is no way that you can do everything. Have an agency system and process to deliver your efficient plan. Do not build a complex ABM plan that you will not run.

Good news: Being an expert or specialist with a managed thought leadership program will make your ABM program much more efficient while waiting for inbound efforts to mature.

ABM = Direct Marketing = Sales

Account-based marketing is a broad subject. Here are some topline thoughts and actions. Your mileage may vary.

But, but, here is where your mileage is irrelevant. According to the 2023 RSW/US New Year Outlook Report where it questioned the clients that you want:

> How do you most often learn about new agencies?
>
> A significant number (44%) stated that they learn about agencies via direct agency outreach.

I'd say 44% is a rather directional response.

Every B2B marketer interested in doing account-based marketing should ask seven key questions:
1. How do I leverage ABM's direct marketing prowess to tell my story and deliver my sales proposition?

2. What are my future clients' pain points? How can I address them to look like a high-value problem solver and leader? How can I personalize my messaging?
3. What tone of voice should I use? What is the balance between and professional and personal? Between rational and emotional marketing? Using humor to stand out works.
4. How can your outbound marketing be unignorable? Consider that the alternative is being ignored.
5. How do I go direct? What text, audio, and video channels should I use? Are there any market gaps I can fill? Testing and data analysis are critical.
6. How do I develop and manage the cadence of my touches?
7. What is the best timing? There is a lot of research on the best day and hour timing for each outbound platform. Some advice is contradictory. You'll need to test for yourself. One of my marketing timing issues is that I've had clients on six continents. The perfect 4PM in California is 5:30AM in Delhi.

The Art of Prospecting

There is no ABM without building an individual, company, or industry category prospect list for your direct marketing program.

Using a dating metaphor: Prospecting is the difference between a 1950s ingénue anxiously waiting for the phone to ring with a call from Mr. Right and today's assertive daters who get out of the house to meet people (or actively use Bumble or Hinge).

The first step in outbound marketing is conducting a client prospect assessment that leads to list building. The process of building a list of your agency's most cherished future clients will focus your efforts.

Create your ideal customer profile (ICP). Who is in your business development B2B sweet spot?

Go one to one: Target primary decision makers with a valuable personalized message. For example, the vice president and global brand leader at Ritz-Carlton should want to read your qualitative study of how competitive hotel brands are using social and paid media. This same study can be sent to individuals across Ritz-Carlton's marketing group.

Go one to many: Do you want a large master list for generalized outbound? Your ABM opportunity here is to deliver category knowledge and insights that would be of value across an industry. For example, all CMOs and marketing teams at large hospitality companies might be interested in your quarterly travel poll, person-on-the-street interviews, and impossible-to-resist newsletter.

Selection criteria includes the following:

1. Establish your sales goals and review the scope of your total addressable market (TAM).
2. Research master categories and industries that you have expert street cred in. Examine subcategories. Zero in. For example, if you are a hospitality expert, a narrow focus might prioritize resorts or spas.
3. Create buyer personas. Key in on the demographics: occupation, job titles, experience and stage of life, interests, pain points and fears, challenges, education, and geography. Isolate emotional needs.
4. Locate prospects with marketing budgets. Target clients currently at other agencies—they spend on advertising programs.
5. Go more horizontal than just the marketing department. Today, CFOs, COOs, and procurement execs should be included on your list. A CFO would be interested in data about social ROI.
6. Locate clients that clearly need help. Find those challenger brands.
7. Think about every person and company that you (and your staff) have interacted with in the past. Stay in touch with past clients who have moved on to another job.
8. Use Google Alerts to keep abreast of people, industry, or individual company news. Like where that CMO just landed.

9. Use services like ZoomInfo, LinkedIn Sales Navigator, Winmo, and the Ratti Report to find that brand new CMO.

Create a rating system to select the best client opportunities based on your business objectives and history. Be realistic, but why not go for it?

Keep all eyes and ears open for opportunities—everyone at the agency, your "partners," should understand the agency's objectives and be visualizing opportunities.

Building the list takes time.

Be efficient and find the right person to build the list. You can do this in-house or outsource to a local intern or a Fiverr assistant.

Use your CRM to keep the list up to date.

Leverage Buyer Intent

I love the idea of acting on buyer intent.

From Gartner:
> What is intent data, and how is it collected? Intent data is a dataset of prospects' behavioral information that indicates what they are interested in and what they are likely to do or buy next. Buyer intent data is collected by analyzing prospects' actions expressing their needs.

A nuts-and-bolts indication of buyer intent could come from content consumption tracking: whitepaper downloads, email newsletter subscribers, and LinkedIn views of your posts, to name a few. Go beyond you to look at the market's reaction to and participation in your competitor's social media.

ZoomInfo can add a direct look at buyer intent via their company and executive tracking. Tracking includes knowing which prospects are actively researching relevant topics on third-party websites.

CHAPTER 12

I view this as being a big WOW worth testing.

ABM Timing & Cadence

A big question I get is, what timing and cadence should be used for outbound messaging to prospects? How many touches do I use, and when?

My Bottom-Line Take on ABM Outreach

Remember that you are sending messages (email or LinkedIn or mail) to strangers. Strangers who, in most cases, don't know you and don't want to hear from you—until they do.

Always keep clutter in mind. The average person receives 100 emails a day. Be succinct. Be relevant. Be personable.

Do not send out lame emails. I am not even going to go into this issue. You know what I'm talking about because you get these every day.

One of your brilliant emails probably won't move the buyer needle. Patience is an ABM virtue. Keep at it. Pleasant persistence wrapped in intelligent must-read information will eventually yield a new contact. Too many agencies send out a limited series and because there wasn't enough action, they can the program too soon.

A smart client who needs you will pay attention to a brilliant business-driving thought leadership insight that provides a clear way for them to advance their business. However, it may take a few varied touches to get the prospect to say let's talk.

A less than ideal prospect will ignore you even if they need you. Maybe they are too focused on losing their job or are in a bad marriage. These guys might never pay attention. And might not have enough gray matter for your agency.

Back to patience. Many prospects do eventually circle back. I get this incoming message often: "I have been reading your stuff for a couple of years and I am ready to talk."

"I am ready to talk" means you are on the prospect's timetable, not yours. If you fade always and aren't there when they're ready, then your efforts have failed.

Timing and a Sample Contact Plan

There is no perfect contact plan. Test alternative approaches.

Consider a 90-day base plan that includes five plus super insight-oriented touches. Do not overwhelm. But nail the objective of creating awareness that you exist and would be a strategic and creative thinking partner. Ongoing research studies and polls can provide strategic message frequency.

Clients are people. Good news: You've built those client personas to understand the company and the person. Visualize what the prospect looks like, how they feel, and what they need—and how they might consume information.

Perform the pain point research required to determine the best relevant information for each type of prospect and category. Use the tools that tell you what works for your competition and just make what they do better. Be opiniated. Ubersuggest is a sweet competitive research tool.

Use your existing market knowledge and stay tuned in: Google Alerts and Trends will let know what issues and opportunities are trending. Is there a perfect content distribution plan? No. But get going, and once you start to roll out your ABM program you will see patterns that can be tossed or repeated.

Here's a starter contact scenario for LinkedIn and email. Consider this a thought starter. Everyone will have their own business objectives, outreach style and voice.

Cadence Management

One of my clients uses the following email and LinkedIn Navigator introduction system to get early-stage meetings with high-quality prospects. To demonstrate their outreach cadence, let's use the idea that the agency is looking for new contacts and relationships in the hospitality category and that it has built a set of valuable insights.

Email 1: Personalize. Add a relevant and timely discovery from your research. For example, "I saw that you opened a new hotel in Cancun. We have experience in the Yucatan and do SEM work for Marriott. Here is a brief case history. Can we set up an appointment to talk about how we delivered positive ROI?" The push for a meeting might be early overkill or not. You decide.

Email 2: Four days later: add "Even more hospitality marketing… I'd like to show you how I helped Mexico Tourism with its marketing." Delivering value offsets friction.

Email 3, seven days later: Add even more value… Offer a brilliant hospitality industry insight to add undeniable value. Have an opinion on why Hyatt is prioritizing luxe while Hilton is adding family vacation options.

It helps if you send something unignorable. For example, research related to a category competition review usually gets attention. My agency did a deep quantitative study of major health-care brands to compare how each used social media. Reading the comparative data was irresistible. This program won us business.

Why not invite the prospect to a high-value webinar? Gotta be high value. In 2013 it could be about AI and hotel selection. In 2024 and beyond… find the latest head scratcher.

Email 4: "Megan, I recognize that our experience might not be a priority right now. However, we'd like to continue to share our expert strategies in the future. I'll stay in touch as we roll out hospitality marketing insights."

Important: Keep at it with class. Periodically send more insights or research. It could take months and even years to get the Marketing Qualified Lead (MQL) hand to raise. It's called sales pressure. Gentle pressure. OK. Not pressure but think of it as sending unignorable thinking to the right target market on a scheduled roll-out basis.

Manage via a content calendar. Really, what do you have to lose unless the prospect screams, "ENOUGH!"

To get past the same old, mix it up. Think about mixing up digital platforms, even getting past digital itself. As I've mentioned, use paper. Use creative insight packaging.

Think about adding in a follow-up after hours voice mail to the prospect—to their company system. Why not make sure that the busy prospect knows that you sent that valuable research?

Wait a few weeks and repeat. Use your CRM tool to keep track of contact outreach. Patience, please. Do not go to sleep.

CHAPTER 13

CHAPTER 13

Inbound Marketing

It's All about Attraction

Inbound marketing is an attraction strategy based on irresistible content marketing that helps clients find you.

Irresistible = unignorable.

Your inbound program should actively attract 24/7 traffic to your brilliant thinking and offers. The goal is to effectively convert this traffic to leads and meetings.

In Chapter 4 I said that you need to be where clients are actively looking for you. If that Hilton Hotel CMO is searching for hospitality marketing news, be there. If they have a specific marketing need that you can address, get it into a searchable blog, Tweet or podcast.

The downside... inbound marketing can become way complex and very time consuming. And it has become less effective over the years. Just wait for the barrage of AI generated blog posts. Yet it still works if you go for being unignorable.

There is a valuable secondary benefit to doing inbound marketing. It's important to note that clients are looking for agencies that have a deep understanding of how to do inbound social and content marketing. Your inbound marketing program will serve as proof of your expertise. Walking the inbound or SEM talk is a good thing.

Be attractive

Be totally focused on knowing what the market wants and needs. A positive tactic to increase inbound traffic is to learn from your competitors. What works for them?

Use tools like Ubersuggest and Similarweb to see what competitive agencies are writing about and do it better.

Get that intern to study what competitive LinkedIn post get liked and shared.

Read the trade press to see what issues they are pushing. Use Google Trends and Alerts. Have an intern do a review of what a trade publication like *Ad Age* is writing about.

Inbound Tactics

Yes, create that valuable agency blog, newsletter, video, and podcast. Better yet, be a guest.

Make sure you've researched the competitive landscape—that is, analyze keywords that drive action, find the information gaps you can address with your expertise and opinions, and concentrate on key industry and CMO issues.

We know smart inbound marketing works—if you work it hard. However, there is additional efficiency to be had. Yes, back to sandwiching ABM and inbound. Your white paper industry study, your interviews, your podcasts can all be sliced and diced and amplified across all the inbound platforms.

Repurposing and amplification options should be embraced.

A Wide-Open Inbound Opportunity

Own a Business Category

Why are industry and category information hubs "owned" only by associations, conferences, and related news websites? Why can't your agency be the category information leader?

Here's an underused inbound content idea: Own your business category's detailed information website, microsite, Instagram (and thus the category).

Use the underused (in the advertising world) listicle, a list-based format that is based on a specific theme.

Want accounts in the hospitality category? Then go out and become its most trusted expert resource.

Build that go-to industry directory. Become positioned as a leader who is a category resource. This acts as a nice 24/7 viewership magnet that positions you as a leader. Optimize the heck out of it.

What might your directory be if you want to own the hospitality category? A hard to resist title: "The Hospitality Industry Navigator."

What are the ingredients?
1. List hospitality news websites. All information in one place.
2. Isolate one major story each week. Remember the 2023 holiday season Southwest Airlines meltdown? You could have written about a marketing plan that would save the airline's reputation.
3. List essential business and marketing white papers. Use a PDF search on Google to find big thinkers.
4. List industry events. Global and regional.
5. List industry awards. Let the winner know that they are on the micro site.

6. Review industry websites.
7. Review new industry marketing programs (Marriot will want to read about Hilton).
8. Highlight primary and secondary industry research.
9. Collate important academic papers.
10. List industry podcasts.
11. Do profiles of industry leaders (including your prospects). Hmm, that should generate some agency awareness.
12. List who is moving to another company. Run those Google Alerts.

Owning the category will help you be positioned as the knowledgeable expert and as a helpful and caring brand.

Drive continuous traffic. Keep the microsite up to date with fresh info. There is something new every month that a brand might find interesting.

Make it an active destination that proves your industry experience, expertise, and digital chops. I have one on my blog and it gets shared. Visit "The Big Advertising Agency Resource List."

Add a newsletter.

Have A Public Relations Plan

Few inbound platforms deliver the positive awareness of having your agency mentioned in a *Campaign* Magazine or *Ad Age* article, or in the case of driving hospitality industry awareness, a magazine like *Hotel Business*.

So how does an agency or agency leader get into the right publication with the right brand-building copy? To find out, I asked Doug Zanger, a former editor of *Adweek*, director of brand and purpose communications at the Martin Agency, and now a consultant for agencies on how to get wonderful trade press attention. Look him up. He is now counseling agencies on their PR planning.

Understand that the publications that you want to be in need you too. This is a symbiotic relationship. Editors and their journalists must fill up their pages every day. They need the right copy to keep the attention of their readers. They need you.

An Editor's PR Advice

You are not alone in seeking press attention. *Adweek* editor Doug Zanger received dozens of incoming agency pitches every week.

He told me that most were ineffective and offered little value. Too many were one-offs and not a strategic relationship-building effort. Too haphazard.

Doug's advice?
1. Have a one-on-one direct marketing plan to drive your brand awareness at the publications the same way you contact future agency clients. Do the research, find a journalist's hot buttons, deliver value and a hard-to-ignore POV. Go slow to build the relationship.
2. Use Muck Rack to build out a list of relevant publications and journalists—like Jamison Fleming, *Adweek*'s managing editor—and agencies and marketing. Study his beat, perspective, personal history, and past articles. What could you say or send that might turn him on?

    Have clear objectives for what you want. Be an authoritative and credible voice on industry trends or breaking news. Doug once interviewed me for an article about the Richards Group's flameout because he knew I was a business development expert.

    Get your fabulous new Marriot campaign in the mags. Get new hires or major promotions in the publications. Are you under 40? Then try to get on the under 40 list. Hmm, why is it always under 40?

    If you want one of those nice awards, you must have a plan

to get the attention of the publication's judges. I asked Doug why I keep seeing the same agencies repeated year to year. He said that it often came down to agency branding and that leading agencies know how to get the attention of the right journalists. If you're out of sight, you're out of mind.

You should study what the award judges are looking for. Importantly, this goes beyond the awards, as the following list is an indication of what the publication views as ongoing leadership subjects. This is what Adweek says about how it selects winners:

> To select Adweek's winners, a diverse jury of editors and writers from across the newsroom gathered to debate two to four finalists in each category. Our discussions focused on a number of factors, including:
>
> How much did the agency grow its revenue? Where did that growth come from? What clients did the agency win or lose?
>
> Did the agency bring in top talent to bolster the shop?
>
> Is the agency taking real steps to retain talent, including nurturing and promoting diverse talent? Is the agency helping build pipelines for underrepresented groups that the whole industry will benefit from?
>
> With sustainability growing ever important, is the agency supporting sustainable growth and helping clients with strategy to become more eco-conscious?
>
> Is this agency a role model for how other agencies should operate?
>
> And most importantly, we look at the creative work. Does

it get us excited about advertising? Does it deliver results? Is it well-crafted with strong strategical insights?

A Bit More PR Advice

The PR firm NATA offers this simple path to quickly get the attention of the busy (as in inundated) press by keeping the messaging straight and to the point. A few words can deliver a big message via being on point and clutter-free. NATA's advice:

> If you run a company or have a job, you almost certainly have to write emails every day. Telling your story should be just as easy as your regular discussions with clients or suppliers.
>
> We've developed a point-by-point technique at NATA PR that helps us get straight to the point when we're talking to journalists or influencers. The purpose of this technique is to make information easy to read and maximize the chances of a journalist talking about you.
>
> Practice this technique using these simple questions. Answer them and then remove the questions before sending your email:
>
> **What:**
> - Brand Z is launching a new vitamin C serum.
>
> **Why:**
> - The vitamin C doesn't become oxidized and retains all its properties that help reduce skin pigmentation.
> - It's a completely new patent from company Z and they are the only ones in the world that have it.
>
> **When:**
> - It'll be launched on X.

Where:
- On Z's website and in reputable pharmacies.

Contact:
- Please don't hesitate to get in touch if you have any questions.

Create or Appear on Podcasts

Podcasts have legs. Smart podcasters promote their episodes via audio and transcribed text on their website and across other platforms. The sweet benefit of podcasts is that you can entice your guests to promote their interview across their own universe to deliver uber amplification and back links.

Remember the goal of being a podcast guest. Guesting = borrowed audience.

And, as mentioned earlier, some podcasts take advertising.

Publish Short Videos

Short videos get found and shared. LinkedIn prefers video to text. There are far fewer videos than blog posts. Google wants to highlight your videos.

Databox reports that 74% of respondents said that videos are more Go to industry events to get your face out there.

Running a PR plan isn't a freebie. However, being mentioned in the trade press is invaluable.

CHAPTER 14

Marketing Insight Distribution

You've got it all together. Your agency's business objectives, positioning, experience, defined target market and lots of brilliant, impossible to ignore thinking. Here's how to get your thought leadership, innovative perspectives, insights (or whatever you want to call it) in front of the right people.

I need to mention a couple of primary distribution objectives first.

Reach. You want your messaging to reach the right decision makers (and their teams). Building a prospecting system is critical.

Frequency. You need to craft an effective approach to how to build the message frequency of your outreach touches. There is no one-size-fits-all cadence/sequencing system. YMMV. Test and keep on testing. The frequent delivery of smartness will grow your pipeline.

Uniqueness. You want to look and sound different than your competitors. Be unignorable.

CHAPTER 14

Think 360-marketing. The term 360-degree marketing was coined around 2000. It recognizes that no single message or platform is enough to make a meaningful dent in an over saturated B2B marketing environment.

Deliver The Insights

1. Your website is your information centerstage. You know that. Why are agency people so obsessed with their websites? Here are some rather compelling numbers to support our obsession.

    Google and Millward Brown Digital reported that 89% of B2B researchers use the internet during their research process and on average conduct 12 searches before engaging with a brand or company. As support, a study by Demand Gen Report found that 77% of B2B buyers said they used a company's website to research a purchase decision.

    Marketing agency websites deliver their thinking via text and video blogs, white papers, webinars, podcasts, and that irresistible study.

2. Landing pages allow the agency to pinpoint a target audience to deliver a discreet message and offer that the visitor can't refuse. This is where you can show off your expertise in a particular category.

3. Email newsletters deliver continuous engagement. Build your list via website offers and gentle outreach. I've employed contractors in the Philippines to help compile mailing lists. Yes, I know about opt in.

Keep your newsletter brief. My agency's newsletter was called *One Idea*. One big idea a month. One idea is perfect for low-attention-span CMOs.

An option: Publish a LinkedIn newsletter. Your connections and followers will be invited to subscribe, and LinkedIn will alert your network whenever you publish new editions.

Another cooler option: You could send out the newsletter as a quarterly zine. Paper is unexpected and works hard.

4. LinkedIn. Post frequently on LinkedIn's personal and company pages (LinkedIn loves video). Put your thinking in LinkedIn groups (I am a member of the Digital Marketing group, which has 2 million members).

    Use LinkedIn Navigator to make direct connections.

    Interreact with your prospect's posts. They will notice that you are smart and pay attention – to them. Be cool, not stalkerish.

5. The other guys. Since every agency and one-person shop and their future client types are different, it is worth testing marketing on the other guys. Facebook, Instagram, Twitter and short-form video platforms are all viable options.

6. B2B advertising. Whoa! Advertising works. These days, given competitive SEM and thought leadership pressure, pay to play has become essential. I know, I know. I know that you know that advertising works. You are an agency after all. However, too many agencies don't even think of advertising their services.

    The agency LONDON Advertising advertises LONDON

CHAPTER 14

Advertising. Go figure. From a Sky News story:

An advertising agency launching a new advertising campaign is nothing new, but it is when the campaign is for rather unusual clients themselves. LONDON Advertising has launched adverts on billboards and TV that include voiceovers from Liam Neeson and Helen Mirren.

From Paul Bainsfair, director general, IPA (UK):

When the London advertising campaign broke, I had to smile to myself because here was an example of an advertising agency doing what most advertising agencies should be telling their clients to do.

Remember to build press love. Sky News even interviewed me for an article about LONDON's advertising program:

When you're an agency that uses advertising, believe me, for some crazy reason you are unignorable.

There are multiple advertising options: PPC on Google and, who knows, maybe include Bing. Test advertising on LinkedIn, Twitter, in client category publications, and ad world directory advertising (e.g., Clutch and Agency Spotter).

Go micro targeting. Why not have agency ads at the top of results for any relevant client company or CEO, COO, or CFO director search? It might be a bit hard for the CMO of Hilton to not notice the ad from you on his very own result page. It would help if he was a narcissist. Many CMOs are.

7. Remarket. Since advertising agency outreach generally needs

more than one touch to nudge conversions, leverage the efficiency of remarketing or retargeting. A rather efficient, low-cost tactic to drive frequency.

8. Podcast advertising. Have you considered running agency business development ads on targeted podcasts? Podcast advertising is booming because it works. It's more difficult to move away from a podcast ad than to click past a *banner* ad.

9. Leverage other people's audience. Why work to build audience when you can borrow it? Guest blog. Guest podcast. Speak at that special conference.

   Start with going guest across some podcasts. Do the legwork to find the best targeted podcasts. Search on Google Podcasts. Consider using a third-party podcast talent agency like Interview Valet to run your podcast selection and outreach.

   Build a list of relevant marketing influencers. Reach out. Pay for play.

10. Artificial Intelligence marketing. AI driven search might be the best search option going forward. How will we optimize for AI? Too early to tell.

11. Go video. Australia's Tiny Hunter agency has over 200 marketing and advertising insight videos on YouTube. The agency tells me that the videos help them close deals with the right new clients—clients who spend time listening to Tiny Hunter's advice. The agency's founders are more interested in closing client relationships than racking up huge indiscriminate view numbers.

CHAPTER 14

12. Publish your book. Books are proof of expertise. My advice: self-publish. There is no need to use a time-consuming traditional publisher if you want to write and distribute that B2B book. My first agency advice book has netted me well over $100,000 in sales and new business.

13. Meet real people at conferences. Go where your next client hangs out. Give that insight talk and make friends. Hand out your book or at least a zine.

14. Direct marketing. I'm thinking old fashioned here. Why not send out #10 envelopes with intriguing insights? Or, as I've mentioned more than once, a well-designed zine.

15. Use the telephone. Warmly.

If there is a sales term that really freaks advertising people out it's *cold calling*.

Cold calling = yuck. And it should. A marketing decision maker does not want a cold call.

But, but, let's think of making that call another way—a process I'd much rather refer to as warm calling.

I say *warm calling* because the warm call would be a follow-up to you sending something valuable (like that mind-blowing man-on-the-street interview video) to a prospect. Or make that call after you know that the prospect demonstrated intent because they opened an email and viewed your newsletter, reacted to a blog post, or viewed your LinkedIn profile.

Some agency folks are afraid of making a smart call—even a warm call.

Here's a warmup: Try calling at off hours (to the office phone of course) and leave a brief voice mail message about your new study. Consider this a light warm touch. More frequency for your messaging.

MARKETING INSIGHT DISTRIBUTION

My Distribution Bottom-Line = Grow Wantedness

I wake up thinking that the client I want... the one that wants to work with me will pay attention to my insights if I get it in front of them. The clients I want, want me to get me in front of them.

CHAPTER 15

CHAPTER 15

Process Wins

Process Rules Business Development. Full Stop.

Understatement: Running a business development program requires tender loving care. Without dedicated oversight, chaos rules.
   Establish a system.
1. Define 12-month business objectives, goals, and potential obstacles.
2. Establish key performance indicators (KPIs).
3. Write mission and vision statements.
4. Build an expert, stand-out agency positioning.
5. Identify key prospects and build a list management system.
6. Review branding elements, including website.
7. Determine your marketing channel roadmap. Research and

develop a kick-ass thought leadership content plan.
8. Develop thought leadership content.
9. Agree on inbound marketing and ABM strategies and distribution tactics.
10. Think about how to have your presence be 24/7.
11. Establish clear responsibilities.
12. Make sure that agency staff recognizes the critical nature of the business development program. This comes from the top.
13. Manage the calendar.
14. Manage your CRM system.
15. Track success metrics. Track website analytics.
16. Have a system to judge what leads are valuable; what RFPs to respond to and what pitches are worth your time and effort. Since there are so many moving parts to making the all-important GO decision, I developed a quick handy-dandy quiz that you and your senior team can take to help you to decide if you really want to spend the time and money to pitch this account. The quiz will even start to help you think through what you will need to say and do to win the business. The quiz is in Resources.

Efficiency is key. Establishing agency systems and processes is imperative in building and running efficient agency business development programs. Today, it is especially important to manage the workload and reduce the potential of staff burnout.

Internal business development–related communications must be carefully managed. Agency staff who touch the business development process should understand the value of business development, the fact that lead generation is critical, and that you have a business development management system that is baked into agency culture. Ensure that everyone knows how valuable their contribution is.

Keep biz dev burnout in mind. Back-to-back RFP responses, etc. are not good for morale.

Your Agency Is Your Client

This is a must. Treat business development as if it were a client. Get past that shoemaker's too busy BS.

Give your program job numbers and personnel assignments. And deadlines.

If you back-burner business development, you will back-burner growth.

Two Management Tools

CRM

Have a customer relationship management (CRM) system to manage your agency's relationships and interactions.

CRM provides a range of benefits:
- A CRM system provides an ongoing business development database and system that can be shared across agency functions.
- It provides management with a global view of prospecting and lead nurturing activities.
- It is a repository for existing leads and lead management. Lead follow-up and lead nurturing will be closely managed.
- It will help you understand prospect triggers. You should know how clients first landed on your website and requested an FRI or RFP, and what specific marketing platform made them make contact.

The real key to reaping the benefits of a CRM tool is using it. Especially true when you never know when your current business development leader will leave your agency, with lots of historical info in their head.

CRM can be a pain in the ass to run and manage. A complex system, think Salesforce, can be overkill for a small agency.

That said, even a weekly updated spreadsheet works better than having no CRM system. Or worse, a CRM system that you're paying for and not using (if so, don't feel bad—most companies that have paid lots for a Salesforce type tool don't use most of its functions).

Consider CRM training across agency functions. Do not have the business development director be the only staff member who knows how to use the CRM system.

Use a Business Development Calendar

The biggest new business program fail is that marketers are not consistent. Start and stop programs don't work.

Calendars are critical to staying on track. As important is that you use it to hold biz dev–related staff, including the business development director, accountable.

List the actions, including who is responsible for getting business development jobs done and out. Clear responsibilities, assignments, and deadlines are required. You do this for client jobs, so do them for your agency to stay on course.

Use the calendar to ensure consistency. Now that you have a prospect list, it's important that you keep your messaging front and center on a scheduled basis. You never know when a target prospect will have a new project for you or will wake up in the middle of the night worrying about their marketing. iPad usage at 3 AM is growing.

Social media content development itself demands a calendar. The calendar demands that you have a content development strategy and plan. Don't be in the position where you ask, "Yikes, what should I post this week?" Do some batch thinking and production to reduce workload.

There are over automated 25 content calendar tools to make this effort easy. LOL. Well, easier. I've written hundreds of blog posts and newsletters. I use a notebook.

CHAPTER 16

Agency Talent Management

It's the People, Stupid

"It's the economy, stupid" was a phrase, a mantra, coined by James Carville in 1992 when he was advising Bill Clinton in his successful run for the White House. It forced the campaign to focus on a key message: it's the economy.

Agencies need to focus on talent management. It's the people, stupid.

Today we are dealing with remote workers, limited days in the office, and an evolving understanding of what working even means.

I stress *evolving*. Some talent-related terms that were not in daily use pre-pandemic:
- Remote working is now universal
- Virtual office
- WFH
- Hybrid work

- Burnout
- Quit quitting
- Quittageon (quitting can become contagious)
- The great resignation
- Resenteeism
- Proximity bias
- Triple-peak syndrome

These terms are just the icing on the workplace cake. Agency management must juggle corporate needs, employee needs, and even client needs as they are also living in the new wildly evolving world of work.

The Art of Retention

Retaining your best people, managing in-house and remote workers, and navigating shifting workplace issues ain't easy. Think about generational differences: how people communicate, what they value in a job, what life-stage they are in.

There is a generation gap. Gen X has different values than Gen Z. I see a few ways to span the gap.

1. Drive intergenerational dialogue and teamwork. Consider break-out group discussions. Get any negatives out on the table. Yes, this can be painful. Group bitch sessions should be avoided. Maybe having one-on-one discussions is a smarter approach. Brevity rules here.
2. Understand how different generations use communications technology. I once had an account executive that only used email to communicate with clients. I suggested that the telephone was a touch more immediate. Today Gen Z appears to prefer Slack to email.
3. Communicate and share agency values and culture.

4. Emphasize interpersonal respect.
5. Develop and consciously manage a mentorship system.
6. Run training programs. Keep them brief.

To Remote or Not to Remote?

"Our assets walk out of the door each evening; we have to make sure that they come back the next morning" said Infosys chairman emeritus Narayana Murthy.

Does this sound familiar? Of course. This is what happens at every advertising agency every day. Your assets are your people.

OK, let's get this obvious fact over with: how we work has changed. Big time.

After 2020 the move to working from home, or Costa Rica, many agency employees simply do not want to return to the office full-time. Ever.

In fact, when we say *remote* work, as in working from home, we could just as easily be saying that returning to an office location is itself remote work after a year or two of working from home and not commuting.

A May 2022 survey of 1,000 US adults found that 39% would consider quitting their jobs if employers are not open to some form of remote work. That number ticks up to 49% for millennials and Gen Z.

I know of a Dallas agency that had senior staff leave to start a new agency simply because their current agency mandated that they return to the office five days a week.

As a result of this tumult, agencies are reviewing how to manage where and when their employees will work—and how they will collaborate. Go back to the office full-time? Part-time? Never? Pick one:

1. Never return to the office. Close the office. Pocket the rent money. The international agency R/GA just did this.
2. Run a hybrid two-office-days-a-week model.
3. Three days a week. Four days a week?

4. Work at the office 60% of the time. Employees get to pick their own timing. Um, a bad idea.

Your agency, either through leader mandate or, better, leadership and employee dialogue, needs a plan. You will need to be flexible and open to even more change because who knows what's coming down the road.

The plan will recognize your geography and its effect on commuting and personal needs like childcare (parents need some flexibility). Every office and geographic location differ. Add in long-distance remote staff and things get rather complicated. Therefore, review your agency's office plan every few months.

But, but. Note that whipsaw office planning can be very debilitating. Make some decisions that will help staff know where and how they will live their life.

Uncertainty sucks.

Burnout Ain't Good

The idea of advertising agency people burnout is not a new thing. A study in 1956 by Life Extension Examiners of New York compared the health of executives in manufacturing, banking, and advertising.

> The ad people showed up worst in 10 of 18 categories, including high blood pressure, organic heart and prostate problems, and abnormal blood counts.

> From 1949 to 1959, at a time when life expectancy for White males was 67.1 years, the average age at death in *Advertising Age*'s obituaries was 59.9. "It's a killing business," concluded Lou Wasey, 71 years old in 1956. "Most of the men who have been along with me in business—they're all dead, and they were younger than I."

Wait a second... I need to repeat this alarming fact: From 1949 to 1959, at a time when life expectancy for White males was 67.1 years, the average age at death in *Advertising Age*'s obituaries was 59.9.

Somehow, I made it past 59.9. Good thing I sold my agency when I did.

Advertising is simply a demanding service business that has gotten much more demanding from a time perspective with the proliferation of needy 24/7 digital programs. The 1949 to 1989 adman had to plan only for TV, radio, print, and out of home. And where the best martinis lived.

Burnout Defined

According to the Mayo Clinic,

> Job burnout is a special type of work-related stress—a state of physical or emotional exhaustion that also involves a sense of reduced accomplishment and loss of personal identity.

It is imperative that agency management understands and knows how to see burnout symptoms before it is too late. Job burnout is endemic in the advertising industry. I'd even say endemic in most service industries.

What Leads to Burnout?

Christina Maslach, a psychology professor at UC Berkeley and the foremost burnout researcher in the United States, names six elements of workplace burnout that management should be conscious of:

- Workload, or being overworked
- Lack of control, or feeling like one lacks resources, decision-making power, and autonomy
- Lack of recognition and reward, or feeling like the reward doesn't match the effort
- Lack of community
- Unfairness

- Lack of meaning and misalignment of values
- Today's new workplace requires management consciousness and communication.

Possibly Some Good News (And Not)

Speaking of management work stress consciousness, it's worth the time to see what's happening on a macro basis. Within the marketing universe, your agency's mileage may (will) vary. There is no single agency type, structure, or size. There isn't even a one-size-fits-all time-utilization factor across industries.

I'm betting that it's good news to see that some employees are using their commute times for recreation and family time instead of loading on more work.

OK. Nice thinking. However, Microsoft may have found another work-related issue.

The Loooonger Day = Triple Peak Syndrome

Triple peak is yet another new term related to remote work. What's triple peak?

Microsoft found that its employees had peak work periods before and just after lunch. The pandemic and work from home changed that. Microsoft found that its people added another work peak between 6 and 8 PM:

> Newer data suggests the trend is here to stay. Traditionally, knowledge workers had two productivity peaks in their workday: before lunch and after lunch. But when the pandemic sent so many people into work-from-home mode, a third peak emerged for some in the hours before bedtime. Microsoft researchers have begun referring to this phenomenon as a "triple peak day."

Flexibility is good. Expanding work hours are not.

Today's new workplace requires enhanced management consciousness and internal communications.

We're so Lonely

Allow me to state the obvious: While working remotely has its advantages, it can also be way lonely.

Lonely in the sense that people are working in isolation and aren't hanging out with and directly interacting with workmates, collaborating, and, importantly, living agency culture. Lack of shared culture, shared goals, and just plain having a next-door office coworker to occasionally complain with breeds stress. The missing in-person interaction experience is particularly hard on younger employees, who miss the comradery.

A few years ago, I was toying with an agency model that had a core in-house team (creative, media, digital, production, account management) and dedicated freelancers or contractors. At that time, it was kinda a new approach—an approach that targeted the idea of being lean and agile to manage down costs while maintain quality.

As part of the planning process, I interviewed some of our freelancers. One of the most interesting observations was what I call the Christmas Party gap. A freelancer told me that the hardest part of freelancing was the alone factor. He said that he really missed going to the agency Christmas party.

For him, lonely meant not Christmas partying. Advertising people like people. Advertising people like fun. On many days, being alone ain't fun.

Think about how to foster deeper communication across time zones or around the block.

The Collaboration Problem

A core advertising agency mantra is our belief in the collaborative nature of creating kick-ass advertising solutions. We think the best thinking and work comes from people working together. People-to-people communication sparks magic ideas.

Y'all remember sitting around that conference room table. Or over a coffee in the kitchen. Or hanging at a local agency bar trading big ideas.

David Gross of Anchor Worldwide stated the interpersonal collaboration need clearly:

> Creative development and production require face-to-face collaboration. It's hard to have a brainstorm on a Zoom call.

Is the Zoom problem real? Yes. But learning to interact personally on a Zoom call is also a management challenge that needs to be resolved.

I live in Mexico, and my consultancy has agency clients on five continents. I've also worked across time zones from a range of foreign cities. While I like to be face-to-face, I don't think working at a distance reduced the efficacy of our collaborative working experience. I've learned how to manage distanced relationships. I also find it can often be easier to do the meeting telephonically to reduce Zoom's visual and tech distractions.

But I'm not creating big advertising solutions where a close interpersonal collaborative environment has historically driven success. Art directors and copywriter teams used to sit together in one office. In London their desks faced each other. What is today's equivalent?

Play the people game. Learn how to make those distanced meetings work.

Workplace Solutions

I'm not convinced that the old-fashioned nine-to-five in-office experience itself was that efficient—or sustainable. Many smart agencies recognized this and offered more flexibility way before the pandemic.

My New York agency had a four-day work week in the summer. Our work did not suffer.

Good managers pay attention to people's personal needs and watch for symptoms of being overworked.

Absentee culture begets lost social connection

- A SHRM study of CEOs and HR officers pointed to maintaining culture as the top remote-work challenge. Stating the obvious, remote work impedes the development of shared agency culture and personal connections. Some solutions to consider:
- Have quarterly meetings to review and discuss company values. Be intentional.
- Experiment with social solutions. Find times to have casual conversations or other forms of social engagements. Not so easy as time zones need to be managed. Not so easy if your developers are in Estonia and your copywriters are in Buenos Aires.
- Think about perks. Help to cover at-home tech needs, including laptops, high-speed connectivity, mic, and lighting to improve the quality of Zoom meetings.
- Add new mental wellness benefits. Virtual cocktail hours, anyone?
- Be proactive. Recognize early signs of stress. Reach out to discuss and meet the challenges.

Three Easy People Management Tactics

Schedule frequent performance reviews

To maintain staff motivation and to provide proof that the company cares, consider increasing the frequency of staff reviews. Why not initiate one-on-one dialogue every six months?

Management by Walking Around (MBWA)

Way back in the 1970s, Tom Peters introduced the idea of management by walking around—a type of people management that involves managers taking random, unplanned walks around the office to improve morale, human contact, and unplanned collaboration. Having the boss sit in their corner office all day was deemed a poor management tactic. This is still an issue. In fact, now it's a mega issue to be resolved when we are miles from each other.

One remote MBWA idea is to have managers create open office meeting times. It's a simple way for people to informally connect and discuss issues and opportunities.

Management via Training

Running agency training programs can deliver a smarter and happier staff. It's proof that you care about your people, their career advancement and your search for excellence:

> 74% (of employees) are ready to learn new skills or re-train to remain employable in the future. (PwC, *Workforce of the Future 2030* report).

Consider running concise small-group Zoom-based training sessions (20 to 30 minutes), virtual team-building workshops (why not hire a facilitator?), and the virtual cocktail hour (everybody is their own bartender). Make learning fun. Bring in a mixologist to invent an agency cocktail.

Speaking of cocktails... Y'all might need that new cocktail to help get through some office-life insanities.

Three Ridiculous Insanities

Email and Slack Insanity

How many emails do you get a day? Slack and messenger notifications? Too many. Too many interruptions lead to distraction and lower productivity. And stress.

A Cure
Email is an example of daily insanity. I'm talking about interminable, unnecessary all day and all-night emails. What seems to be an emergency must-act-now email from a colleague on Sunday morning just might not be that urgent.

The agency email system and always-on culture need to be tamed. Management must design internal communication and communication etiquette and rules.

Periodically discuss the magnificent benefit of reducing CC and BCC lists—less is more. Lower expectations for immediate response (unless you get a client request). Have agency correspondence rules. This might be a bit more difficult as people use the CC thing to prove that they are paying attention from their apartment kitchen.

Reduce reply all. Everyone does not need to be in on every Slack dialogue to be concise.

Turn off notifications—especially mobile.

Get past multitasking. Sure, multitaskers like to parade their multi-ness. BS. Don't take my word for it. Neuropsychologist Cynthia Kubu says, "When we think we're multitasking, most often we aren't really doing two things at once. But instead, we're doing individual actions in rapid succession, or task-switching."

Meeting Insanity

How many unnecessary, poorly managed meetings do you sit it? Add in staring at a screen with thumbnail-size talking heads and you can start to feel the burn coming on.

Poorly managed advertising, design, and PR agency meetings waste time, kill creativity, and cost money.

A Cure

My Northwest Airlines client's marketing department had a serious meeting problem. Most of my clients seemed to be in nonstop meetings from 8 AM to 6 PM. I couldn't figure out when they had time to think, let alone get their jobs done.

This fact wasn't lost on the airline's CEO, who hired a management consultant to help create an efficient and effective meeting culture. A culture with stated rules to increase meeting effectives and reduce the length of meetings.

Here are the eight rules I picked up at Northwest:
1. Before booking a meeting room or Zoom window, ask if a face-to-face meeting is even necessary.
2. Designate a meeting leader to run the meeting and manage the process.
3. Have clear objectives and an agenda.
4. Invite only the people who need to be in the meeting. This isn't a numbers game. Well, it is if you calculate the cost of meetings.
5. Show up on time. Keeping colleagues waiting is rude and costly.
6. Have a timetable. Make sure anyone needed in the meeting knows of the start and stop times.
7. End the meeting when you've covered the objectives. No rambling.
8. State any follow-up items, timing, and individual responsibilities. If a meeting needs some memory, send out a brief meeting summary ASAP.

And here it comes: Now a few words from Elon Musk. Of course.
1. "No big meetings." Think about the cost of filling up a room. Five

agency people in a one-hour meeting at a billable rate of $200 per hour costs you $1,000. Ten of those meetings a week will cost you $10,000, or one a week will cost you $52,000 per year.
2. "No frequent meetings."
3. "Leave a meeting if you are not contributing." I love this one. Just get up and go do some real work.

Sage advice all around.

I suggest that agencies develop internal meeting rules. Everyone will be grateful. Burnout will be reduced.

Go further: Share your meeting rules with clients—demonstrate that your agency is well managed. Show them that you care about their time.

Client Insanity

We all want more clients, ever more happy clients who want to work with us forever.

To get to this holy grail, we must take the time to fully understand the client's mindset, goals, and even emotional needs.

Today's marketers live on the 24/7 social marketing hamster wheel. CMOs are on that fast-paced wheel and on a job tenure rollercoaster. The leadership advisory firm Spencer Stuart reported that the average tenure for CMOs is 40 months. Only 3.3 years. The lowest level in more than a decade.

Clients want to show success fast. This results in your people running fast. Probably too fast. You need three Instagram reels a day? You got it. Five Instagram posts this week. Yup, you got it. A review of the Google Ads plan? Yup. A weekly analysis of all related KPI stats? That really big creative idea? Coming right up. And on and on.

Managing the client mindset (real and perceived need) requires real-time consciousness of their objectives and stresses, and an agency system that recognizes that agency-to-client communication is critical.

Take time to review best-of-class client management. Discuss how to listen—and look like you're listening. This is called active listening. Be proactive in periodically discussing your client management systems.

Get past just being order takers. See Chapter 18, Client Management for more.

Manage Boss Burnout

Lots and lots of press and studies exists about how to manage employee burnout. But what about boss burnout?

Bosses, from mega-agencies to one-person companies must contend with changing economic landscapes, 24/7 workloads, the world of projects, client retention, constant pitching, the delivery of excellent agency work, managing the P&L, and fostering staff and partnership happiness. Yikes, that is a lot to juggle that breeds sleepless nights.

It's never good for any size agency to have a stressed-out boss. I've lived it as both an employee and a boss. But don't take my word for it. The *Harvard Business Review* is on the case.

> It's stunning how quickly your stressed-out boss can turn you into a stressed-out team member. This is partly because of the contagious nature of emotions.

Boss stress and resulting burnout is an agency-wide issue. An issue that must be recognized and managed. The boss must pay attention to signals of overstress for their sake and the sake of total agency good vibrations and agency culture.

Before I get into my advice for how to manage boss burnout, I offer some large agency insights from Michael Farmer. Michael is a consultant to agency holding companies, a leading expert in managing agency scope of work and is the author of *Madison Avenue Manslaughter*, easily one of the best advertising book titles ever. Here is my question and Michael's no holds barred answers.

PL: Michael, what are you seeing at the top of the agency pyramid?

Michael: Senior agency executives burnout from the constant losing and winning of new business. A constant cycle of pitching.

They focus on the short-term – the need to make quarterly numbers. It affects their personal compensation.

They have no ideas about how to change things:
- They compete on price with all other agencies.
- Procurement has all the power.
- Holding companies win business at low prices – and they have to participate.
- Their agencies are vendors, rather than partners with their clients.
- They've seen much of their talent liquidated in annual downsizings. They're left with junior resources.

If they knew how to turn things around, they would (they say) – but I don't believe them. I have yet to meet a single agency that kept track of its scopes of work and knew what work was being done on each client.

Without knowing the nature of the work, how can they expect to be partners who make a difference in client performance?

WOW! Yikes!

OK, what about you? Manage *your* boss role.
- Get back to reviewing your agency's business model. How and where do you fit into today's advertising universe? Make necessary adjustments. Make sure that your agency's service offer meets the needs of the market.
- Do not respond to every RFP and pitch request. Use my go-no-go questionnaire in the resources section.
- Take a hard look at current responsibilities and transfer or share ownership where appropriate.

CHAPTER 16

- Connect more personally with your team members. Understand their needs and issues. No, don't have yak sessions where everyone dumps on the boss. However, frank, managed conversations will help to get everyone on the same page to work out any issues. Asking, "How'm I doin'?", worked big time for New York's ex-mayor Ed Koch who asked this question of citizens on his daily walks. A very MBWA guy.
- Take time off. Go work out. Even bosses need that work–life balance.

Bottom line: happy bosses lead to a happier agency and more fun for everyone. And longer careers.

CHAPTER 17

Recruitment

The Art of Recruitment

The advertising industry is experiencing some brain drain. A range of factors has made a career in adverting not look as groovy as Don Draper's Madison Avenue three-martini lunches.

According to WordStream's *State of the Agency* report,

> Hiring is a top-three challenge, and 15% of digital marketing agencies feel that hiring and training new employees is the biggest challenge they will face this year.

Factors leading to advertising's very own brain-drain include:
1. Lower profits. The loss of the golden 15% media commission structure back in the early 1990s put a clamp on agency profits and perks. Selling project man hours versus agency value does

not help foster good vibes either.
2. The 24/7 digital workload. Jay Chiat's *wonderful* line, "If you can't be bothered to work on Saturday, don't bother to come in on Sunday." Ain't cute today. If it ever was.
3. Salary and WFH issues. These days it can look like an agency person can make more bucks as a freelancer. My website designer lives in Portugal. I'm using a video editor in Minneapolis. Some ad biz people jumped ship to the client side. Some experienced agency people would prefer to run a bagel bakery (true) or a brewery.
4. It has taken too long for the industry to help women, minorities, and the LGBTQ+ community to see a clear career path.
5. The pandemic shifted much of the talent job search control to the prospective employee.
6. Every agency is now competing for talent with agencies around the world. If *I* can work from anywhere, I can work for *any* advertising agency anywhere. This makes it important to develop and consciously manage mentorship.

A Well Managed Recruitment Plan

You cannot wait till you need that new employee to create a recruitment plan.

Review your agency brand and culture messaging. Assess how you look and sound. Would *you* want to work for you?

Does your website sell your workplace culture?

Be smart (and creative) about how you describe job openings.

Have clear, as in not vague, job descriptions. Look at competitive agency copy. How can you stand out? Ask yourself, would *you* want to work for you?

Leverage the hell out of LinkedIn as a recruitment tool. One of my clients goes directly to people at other companies who have the required skill sets. This agency has a recruitment enticement script that lays out all the benefits of working at their company. Direct outreach has been the agency's single best-performing recruitment tool.

Think ahead. It is possible to start to meet future employees even before you may need them. Make friends. Be a networker. Always be recruiting. A new term = ABR.

Ensure that all your employees know about the jobs that need to be filled. People know people who know people. Provide staff members (and friends of the agency) with a clear understanding of what you're looking for and how to sell-in the agency if they're a primary early contact.

Recognize that you're dealing with generational differences. Reflect individual needs when discussing your employer brand story. Build the right benefits talking points. Younger employees are looking for different things than baby boomers.

I mentioned generational differences earlier. PwC's *NextGen Survey* found that

> Millennials would select flexible working, work-life balance, and the chance for overseas assignments above financial rewards. Generation Xers are raising families and are understandably the biggest users of flexible working (81%), compared to millennials (56%).

Sell-in the idea that you have a high-value training system to help employees learn and grow. Be able to say, "When you join agency XYZ, we will help you grow."

Shorten the time used for the interview process. That wonderful employee might find their next job halfway through your agency's five-person interview process. Ah hmm... if you invite your people into the interview process, train your staff on how to interview. Get the word out on what to ask and even how to sell the agency. I've hired dozens and was never trained in how best to interview.

CHAPTER 17

The Onboarding Dilemma

Efficient onboarding works for both the new employee and the agency. Have a clear approach to how to onboard workers—especially remote workers.

I have a smart, experienced business development director client who was recently let go from her remote agency business development job. A key reason for termination was that she never had the chance to fully integrate into the company and its culture and have opportunities to form a bond with agency management. According to the SHRM Foundation, the four Cs of traditional onboarding are clarification, compliance, connection, and culture.

Building personal connections and sharing culture, particularly important to agency morale, are rather difficult to manage on a laptop. Jamie Kohn, research director for the HR practice at consulting firm Gartner gets to the point:

Employees today are experiencing a crisis of connection, and HR leaders report that the biggest challenge with expanding remote work is maintaining the organization's culture.

Traditionally, new hires connected to organizational culture organically by living it in their day-to-day, in-person interactions. For many people working remotely, changing companies can feel like swapping out one laptop for another.

Starting my career in a 1,000-person office in New York's iconic Chrysler Building with our own cafeteria, gym, and many local bars and coffee shops built relationships and solidified agency culture. Hard to do today when the copywriter is in Denver and the art director is in Miami.

Onboarding Solutions

Be proactive and aware. Develop a preboarding system that starts the onboarding process ahead of the first day on the job. This is an opportunity to prove your interest in the new employee, introduce them to future colleagues, and begin to cement cultural nuances. The payback can be significant.

Amazon's HR department has pointed out that preboarding increases the retention of first-year employees. Pre-boarding saves money.

Design the onboarding system to get ahead of new employee expectations. Note the rather compelling research responses from *Failure to Attach: The Crisis for Pandemic Hires* by Perceptyx. See how many respondents said yes to this critical onboarding-related statement: "I had a clear understanding of what to expect on my first day as an employee":

Pre-pandemic = 74.9%
During pandemic = 60.7%

Fifteen percentage points is a huge difference. A potentially huge failure. Really, how hard is it to manage expectations? Food for thought…

- Hold personal onboarding sessions for new employees. Include one or more current employees.
- Develop an onboarding kit—agency status and history information and some swag if you've got it.
- Prepare an organization chart. Where will the new hire fit in?
- Foster dialogue. Nurture and plan ongoing one-on-one conversations between new and existing employees since people are not accidently meeting each other in agency public spaces.

How well are you dealing with the new HR world? What is your plan? Play the long game.

CHAPTER 17

The Power of Culture

Defining agency culture has become a serious make-or-break recruitment tool. What are your agency's values? Does it have a purpose beyond just making bucks? How does it manage the work–life balance equation? Is it community minded? Are you charitable? Do you have diversity inclusion initiatives?

What Is Corporate Culture?

Corporate culture is the set of values, beliefs, behaviors, and attitudes that characterize a company and its employees. It's what makes a company unique and is reflected in everything from the way employees interact with each other to the company's core values and mission statement.

A strong corporate culture can be the difference between a company that can attract and retain top talent and one that can't. This is especially true in the case of Gen X and millennials, who place a high value on finding a job with a company that shares their values.

Three reasons why creating a human-oriented culture and vision will deliver success.

1. It attracts top talent. As noted before, corporate culture can be the deciding factor for candidates who are trying to choose between two similar job offers. If Company A's corporate culture appeals to the candidate more than that of Company B, then the candidate is more likely to accept a job offer from Company A. Here's a positive, employee-friendly vision statement from LinkedIn:

    We welcome and seek constructive feedback so we can learn and grow. This is our company, and we operate together against our single vision: to create economic opportunity for every member of the global workforce.

2. It promotes employee retention. Once you've attracted top talent, you want to keep them around. A strong corporate culture can help with employee retention by fostering loyalty and commitment among employees. Employees who feel like they belong to a supportive community are less likely to look for new opportunities elsewhere.
3. A positive culture grips the attention of clients. Clients are humans too.

Yes, have that humanity-based culture and vision. Be like Patagonia or Ben & Jerry's.

Need Proof? Some Research

A study by Glassdoor found that 60% of job seekers would not apply for a job with a company if they didn't like the look of its website, and another study found that 78% of employers believe that a prospective employee's cultural fit is more important than their skill set.

What does this mean? It means that if your company doesn't have a well-defined corporate culture, you're going to have a hard time attracting the best and the brightest. Make sure your culture-speak is represented in actions. Walk that talk.

Seven Culture Thought Starters

Here are some ideas and thought starters to get your advertising agency culture in gear. Riff on these. Discuss the value of each idea. Get internal feedback, read about what works at leading companies, and study your competitors. Defining your culture is not the best area in which to be dictatorial.

1. Write those compelling mission and vision statements to foster alignment.
   Boise's Oliver Russell, a B Corporation agency nails it: "Oliver Russell is a branding agency that elevates the impact of companies

striving to do good for people and our planet." They walk the talk. More. Oliver Russell's Inspiration Alley project is a collection of large-scale murals depicting social justice heroes—Malala Yousafzai, Maya Moore, Colin Kaepernick, and Dolores Huerta. They visualize their vision. Also take a look at the book: *Rise Up: How To Build a Socially Conscious Business* from Oliver Russell's leader Russ Stoddard.

2. Diversity as mission is a key element of the W+K vision: "Our founders, Dan Wieden and David Kennedy, were clear on our mission from the start, "To create a place where people could come and live up their full potential. Where they could do the best work of their career because that place relished freedom, diversity, and unpredictability.'"

3. Tame the long-distance issue. Create scheduled 30-minute meet-and-greet opportunities for new employees. Have department leaders talk about their objectives.

4. Have a platform (in person or digital) that allows employees to share ideas, personal info, and dreams with each other. This can get old so use some of that creative thing to make it valuable and fun.

5. Have offsite team-building meetings. In many cases, this will cost less than keeping all that expensive office space. I live in San Miguel de Allende, Mexico, and according to Conde Nast Traveler it is the friendliest city in the world. Come on down. I'll show you around.

6. Develop a paid employee volunteer program to address community issues. Poll your employees for their opinions about this year's agency charitable work. Walk the talk by being inclusive.

7. Invest in your culture via training and development programs. It will be a triple win. This works for the employee, you the boss, and your clients. Why not invite them to your series of thirty-minute training sessions.

I talk to my ad agency clients about building an advertising agency brand that is unignorable. A brand that stands out from the pack. Culture is a key component. Make your culture unignorable and hard to resist.

Diversity, Equity, and Inclusion

Agencies have gotten past the age of male domination. Statista reported in 2019 that women represent 59.7% of employees at independent agencies. Even more: 51% of CMOs in *Ad Age*'s 2021 top 100 advertisers were women.

There are compelling reasons that driving a more diverse work force needs to be a serious goal of agencies.

Agency staffing should strive to reflect real-world demographics. Period. Should we expect that a White 23-year-old content developer can get in the head of a 46-year-old Latino parent? A few can. But not most.

Diverse agencies make more money. According to MarketingHire,

> McKinsey found companies in the top quartile for gender diversity on executive teams were 21 percent more likely to outperform on profitability and 27 percent more likely to have superior value creation.

> Meanwhile, companies in the top quartile for ethnic/cultural diversity on executive teams were 33 percent more likely to have industry-leading profitability.

If this financial outperformance information doesn't start to nudge you to having an active diversity recruitment program, I'm not sure what would.

Chapter 17

Larger Agencies Get It

R/GA has Cultural Collectives groups to help diverse employees connect. If I were looking at an agency that cares about my personal needs and has a way to connect me to my "group," I'd think that R/GA was walking the talk. R/GA's individual Cultural Collectives include women, Black, Asian, Arabic, Hispanic, and LGBTQ+ groups.

You don't have to be large to make diversity an agency goal. New York's Orchard, at under 50 employees, is another agency that puts it on the table:

> When we founded Orchard in 2019, we made it central to our mission to actively address the issues of gender and racial inequality. We made the following concrete commitments:
>
> Our majority equity shareholder and highest paid employee is and always will be female.
>
> All female employees at orchard are paid equal to or more than their male peers.
>
> We would increase the size of our BIPOC talent pool available to the entire industry in pursuit of which we voluntarily train at-risk BIPOC youth for careers in the communication and media arts.

Does this Orchard statement resonate? The impact of this initiative was acknowledged by Facebook's chief creative officer and VP of global business marketing during Facebook at Cannes Lions Live 2021:

> You can only stand up and talk about things if you're actually doing something about them. An agency we love that has been doing this since 2019 is Orchard. Their story is really inspiring...

Orchard's commitment to their internship program is crucial to ensuring a diverse future in the marketing industry.

Right on, Orchard.

My bottom line here is that the advertising industry must be very active in creating a diverse workforce. Just mouthing the words doesn't cut it.

Actively Recruit the Next Generation

Like Orchard, get out into the community and sell, yes sell, the idea that working in adverting is a smart career choice. Start them thinking early.

My conversations with Black and Hispanic agency owners confirm that the ad industry must work with youth precollege to begin their journey into advertising.

Wil Shelton, CEO of LA's Will Power Integrated Marketing, told me that an issue within the Black community is that advertising is not even a recognized career path. Kids who want to be Stephen Curry or YoungBoy are not thinking of Adolescent's Ramaa Mosle, Mischief's Greg Hahn or RG/A's Robert Greenberg. Get out in the market earlier, meet teens and talk up the benefits of an advertising career. Make a difference. The payback will come.

Once again, walk the talk. It takes only a couple of hours to go to an inner-city school to pitch marketing and advertising as a profession. Excite the next gen. Bring you team along. Bring clients.

If you need a bit of inspiration and an advertising version of Kevin Durant, head over to my *Advertising Stories* podcast interview with L.A.'s Wil Shelton on how his Wil Power Integrated Marketing agency is a super power in the black community.

CHAPTER 17

DE&I Is Good Business

Don't take my word for it. According to McKinsey's *Diversity Wins* report,

> Our 2019 analysis finds that companies in the top quartile for gender diversity on executive teams were 25 percent more likely to have above-average profitability than companies in the fourth quartile—up from 21 percent in 2017 and 15 percent in 2014.

Clients pay attention to an agency's DE&I awareness and structure.

This is particularly evident in the growing number of RFPs that are aimed at women- or minority-owned agencies.

Inclusion Includes the Ageism Issue

Diversity goes beyond racial, ethnic, and LGBTQ+ diversity. Ageism, another business and cultural issue, is a global business challenge.

From *Wikipedia*:

> Ageism, also spelled agism, is discrimination against individuals or groups on the basis of their age. This may be casual or systemic.

Ageism is particularly endemic in the advertising industry. In 2021 only 8% of WPP's workforce was over 50, and rival Dentsu's 50-plus total skewed lower at 6.9%. Note that 34% of the US population is over 50. Simply insane.

Given the size and purchasing power of the 50-plus group, it's amazing how poorly this demographic is properly represented in advertising campaigns. From AARP on the effect of ageism on the advertising product itself:

That helps explain why those age 50 and over who do most of the consumer spending represent only 15 percent of adults in online media images and are seven times more likely than younger adults to be portrayed negatively.

I see two reasons for our age of ageism.

First, there appears to be a belief that younger people are simply better at creating truly wonderful marketing, advertising, and new tech solutions in the digital age.

What does Marc Zuckerberg think? "Young people are just smarter." Think it's just Silicon Valley speak? Nope. Just ask WPP:

> We have a very broad range of skills and if you look at our people—the average age of someone who works at WPP is less than 30—they don't hark back to the 1980s, luckily.

This lame statement was care of WPP's CEO Mark Read. Read is around 55. Guess it's OK for management to be "old."

The second reason for agency ageism is related to the cost of older employees. Employees over 50 simply cost more. Higher costs are not a good thing in a profit-stressed industry like advertising.

In addition to having a higher salary requirement than a twentysomething, older employees have higher employment-related costs. Older employees' benefits like the health plan and longer vacations simply cost more. Growing annual health-care costs was a major reason I decided to sell my advertising agency.

Yes, costs play a huge role. However, advertising is an industry that has decided that youth is a requirement in the digital age. Agencies like natives. Somehow marketing experience delivers less value. Bob Hoffman knows.

> If you think that ageism in advertising is solely a byproduct of agencies having to cut costs, you're wrong. Most agencies

CHAPTER 17

wouldn't hire a 55-year-old copywriter if she came free and gift-wrapped.

I'll end with an interesting stat: US boomers hold $71 trillion in assets. To put this into perspective, one-seventh of the world's assets are controlled by 76 million US boomers.

Does this remarkable stat suggest that agencies will hire more 50-plus employees to help their clients understand, reach, and sell to the older, richer crowd? No.

So, what is really the reason for ageism in advertising? My takeaway is that people over 50 are smart but are just too expensive for a low-margin industry like advertising. Agree?

CHAPTER 18
Community Spirit

Community spirit, as in delivering beneficial philanthropy to local or national organizations, is an active expression of the agency's culture and vision talk. While much corporate giving is centered on monetary donations and sponsorships, advertising agencies of all types are uniquely positioned to provide valuable marketing assistance to not-for-profit entities.

My agency worked closely with Make-A-Wish Oregon. We provided free marketing services and gave cash donations, and I sat on the board. Everybody won: Make-A-Wish, critically ill kids, their parents, the broader community, and our team, who felt good about working at an agency that delivered on our community-oriented vision.

The Art of Philanthropy and Your Ad Agency

Many, but not enough, advertising agencies have one or more nonprofit clients. It can be a wonderfully symbiotic relationship.

This important charitable work also provides benefits for the agency's recruitment and new business programs. If done correctly, the nonprofit relationship is strategic. One agency that gets it is Portland's Grady Britton. You can read about their multi-year program in my HubSpot article "An Agency That Does Good."

I've felt so strongly about the symbiotic aspect of charitable work that I've always recommended a strategic philanthropic approach or plan to my clients. Below is how I've represented this concept. If you agree with me, please pass this on to your clients. At a time of reduced corporate spending, it's important that agencies play a more assertive role in selling the benefits of strategic philanthropy, internally and externally.

Strategic Philanthropy Is Good Business

During recessions, many agencies lower their annual investment in philanthropic donations. Because of this, I believe this is precisely the time to consider why, how, and where you donate based on adopting the principles and benefits of strategic philanthropy. But what is that?

Strategic philanthropy, also known as cause marketing, is a business strategy whereby a company clearly aligns its mission and business goals with those of a nonprofit organization to create a strategically tailored and mutually beneficial partnership. A well-designed program balances the positive impact on the community with a clear understanding of the positive impact a giving program will have for the company, its brand, customers, and, importantly, employee recruitment and retention.

Strategic philanthropy isn't about disguising self-serving activities under a veil of good intentions or adopting a cause simply to sell more products. It is about sincerely showing your clients, customers, and employees that you really care about your community and important causes. It's about having your organization receive measurable benefits that will make you want to donate even more next year. This is a win-win marketing program for your company, your employees, nonprofit partners, and even agency clients.

Why Participate with Nonprofits?
Effective strategic alliances will enhance your brand equity and image, increase stakeholder and employee loyalty, and lead to increased revenue and sales for the parties involved.

It's not difficult to leverage your charitable activities to enhance your corporate image. Here are six thoughts to get you started.

1. Think small.

    Consider working with local charities that can demonstrate in-market impact from your donations.

2. Create alignment.

    Consider aligning your services, and areas of expertise with an organization that complements your company's mission and business.

3. Lead by being a positive example.

    Set up a charitable program with clear community benefits to demonstrate to your employees and clients that your company doesn't exist simply to make money.

4. Involve your employees.

    Build a program that gives your employees a sense of ownership and a direct, visible connection to the good you are doing. Working with local charities will allow your employees to participate on a personal level. Think cultural enhancement.

5. Spread the word.

    Most nonprofits have limited funds for advertising and public relations. Leverage your giving to promote your charitable programs and to help create awareness for your nonprofit partners. Pitch positive community-interest stories to the local press, have a charitable giving section on your website, and let your clients know what you're doing. Don't be shy.

6. Think bottom line.
   If you and other businesses see a tangible benefit from giving, you and they will give more. This may be the most compelling point of all.

Facts to Support the Concept of Strategic Philanthropy
According to the Cone Cause Evolution Study, a national survey on the attitudes of Americans about corporate giving, there are many benefits to be accrued from strategic philanthropy:

88% of Americans say it is acceptable for companies to involve a cause or issue in their marketing. This record number represents a 33% increase since Cone began measuring in 1993 (66%).

85% of consumers have a more positive image of a product or company when it supports a cause they care about.

90% of consumers want companies to tell them the ways they are supporting causes. Put another way: More than 278 million people in the U.S. want to know what a company is doing to benefit a cause.

Giving is a good thing. Making giving sound like a good thing is really a good mission. Telling the world that you live your positive corporate vision is an all-around good thing for your agency.

Giving is especially a good thing if you pitch the art of strategic philanthropy to your clients. Everyone wins.

CHAPTER 19
Client Management

What Do Clients Want?

Your next client probably has multiple needs, even if they think all they need is an Instagram influencer program or seriously good video storytelling.

It's often difficult for a client to clearly state business objectives. Objectives range from increasing sales and revenues; growing brand awareness; building loyalty; new product development; geo expansion to more Xandr please. Just to name a few. I've seen an inability to express clear objectives across client seniority. I once had a senior Nike client who didn't have clearly stated sales goals. I know, kinda crazy.

Instead of asking for those numbers, I asked my client friend how she made her bonus. Interesting revelations in that discussion, including finding out where the agency could act to help make her a Nike star.

Let's look at some industry research to help us get into CMOs' heads.

CHAPTER 19

The UK firm SCOPEN interviewed 81 senior marketing professionals, including 57 chief marketing officers, and 56 agency professionals. The overwhelming majority of respondents (72.8%) were the ultimate spending decision makers. The research showed that creativity is the number one criterion used in agency selection.

However, SCOPEN also reported,

> It's interesting to see how (clients) are talking more about innovation related with business transformation, and digital transformation, which is a different territory from creativity, much more difficult, of course, to find agencies in that space.

I'll parse this out. Here is SCOPEN's list of large client needs.
1. Creativity
2. Innovative ideas (how W+K got that first piece of Ford)
3. Digital capabilities
4. Strategic planning
5. Marketplace insights
6. Competitor insights
7. Brand knowledge
8. Trend awareness and predictions
9. Media planning
10. Social media prowess
11. Integrated services
12. Good value

That's a long list. Not all clients need all of that. To simplify, I believe that most clients are looking for advertising experts. Be the expert who delivers smart, efficient programs plus measurable results. High ROI results.

What Type of Agency Does the Client Need?

Once the client determines their marketing objectives, or thinks they have, they'll think through the type of agency they want to work with. Here's my short list of agency types and how you might position your agency based on pitch-oriented typecasting:

Regional leader
No one knows your local or regional market better than you. Your market-driven local reputation drives your new business success. There are agencies that are asked to every regional or local pitch simply because they have been around forever, know their markets, and thrive on referrals.

Creative hero
Your work stands out, gets discussed, has won awards, and, most importantly, has a history of building brands and market share. Clients want creative agencies (it's an essential part of what we offer), but creativity is in the eye of the beholder and can be difficult to demonstrate—especially when pitching less experienced clients.

Full-service provider
Our industry has gone back and forth on the value of the full-service agency. I sense that we're currently experiencing a shift toward smaller full-service agencies that can deliver an integrated approach. There are so many moving parts to marketing today that some clients are becoming overwhelmed and need a single strategic partner that can help build and manage an integrated plan. Agency selection research backs up the need for integrated solutions.

Strategist
You've developed a reputation for your strategic insights and guidance. You've solved tough client problems in the past and have the cases to

prove it. You offer innovation and live to beat down disruption. You see into the future.

Specialist
You've positioned your agency as an expert. You could be a mobile, SEM, social media, content, experiential, PR, or digital expert. The list of specialization opportunities keeps growing. Pay attention to what's hot, what's next.

Category market expert
You know the client's industry or product category better than any other agency. You've supported this fact with extensive client category history and your leading thought-leadership program.

Target market expert
No agency knows the client's target market, demographics, and consumers better than you.

Big
When I was at Saatchi & Saatchi, we led every pitch with a global map showing all the Saatchi offices. I called it our dot map. We had dots everywhere. Big multinational clients want integrated global services and an agency that can run campaigns across borders. These clients need (or think they need) big networks and lots of dots.

Big is usually a good thing. The downside of big is that mid-size clients can feel like they could get lost inside a huge global agency.

I once solved the too-big client issue by not selling in the huge Saatchi brand. We sold in a bespoke agency setup made up of three agency principles. The agency, Keeshan Jeary and Levitan, offered personalized services plus all the value inherent in the world's largest agency. Big became small and personalized.

Then Again, Small Works

Small Agencies Can Win Large Accounts

A recent interview in *Ad Age*'s *Ad Lib* podcast reveals the insight that even large clients are now attracted to smaller agencies. I'd imagine that this might not be a big surprise to you. Smaller agencies that deliver specialized services have been on client radar for a few years.

Nike hired my small agency to work on Nike's Major League Baseball and college sports marketing programs because of our sports marketing expertise. Not our global reach.

So… What do the big clients want to see from smaller agencies, and is your agency set up to deliver it?

Client Advice for Small Agencies

Maureen Morrison's **Ad Age** article "How a Small Agency Can Land a Big Client Like Mondelez" sheds some light on this universal question. The article is an interview with Mondelez International's agency scout Deb Giampoli. Deb shares her tips on the dos and don'ts of how to get her attention:

> **Do have a story to tell.**
> "Make sure your shop has a compelling story about who you are and what you do. If you want to punch above your weight, have more than a capabilities deck to show."
>
> **Do know how to articulate your strategy and talk about your work.**
> "The bar is just as high for small agencies as it is for big ones," Ms. Giampoli said. "Great work is every agency's best calling card," she added.
>
> **Do make yourself visible.**
> "Approach marketing executives through mutual connections, conferences or writing white papers on interesting topics. If

you're really good at what you do, I will find you… When you do get found, have a great story to tell about who you are and what you do."

Don't cold call potential clients without doing your homework.
Ms. Giampoli said she won't work with an agency that hasn't researched her role and what she values in agencies. If you are going to cold call, she said, the only chance you have is if you've done your homework.

Don't expect a meeting to lead to an immediate assignment.
"I don't believe in love at first sight. I might meet you and like you a lot, but that doesn't mean that something's going to happen quickly."

Don't be a general agency with a mediocre offering.
Ms. Giampoli said, "It's far better to be a shop with a smaller, more specialized offering than a jack-of-all-trades without anything compelling."

She closed the interview with, "I get emails from small agencies all the time apologizing for being small… Don't apologize for being small."

The NBA's Muggsy Bogues was 5'3". He never apologized. Small and smart can be a beautiful thing. Einstein was 5'7". Elliot Page is 5'1".

How Much Should a Client Spend?

When I was a punk account executive on the General Mills new products account, my client's marketing director called me up and asked me how much GMI should spend to launch a new pasta brand. I was like a deer in headlights. No one at the agency had ever prepped me on how to set an advertising budget. I had no clue. I told my client I'd have to get back to them.

For most brands establishing an advertising budget is one of their most difficult decisions. Painful. Even with all those wonderful tracking metrics, I still think that John Wannamaker kinda got it right. You probably know where I'm going:

> Half the money I spend on advertising is wasted; the trouble is I don't know which half.

Of course, the "I don't know which half" message will be denied by quant jocks. But you get the idea and need to keep this client stress-building pain point in mind when talking budgets.

When I eventually ran my own agency, I tried to create a set of budget benchmarks to help with the "how much" question and to try to get past having to super-customize each job. Did we succeed? Well, as a full-service agency, mostly no. Super specialists, à la SEO or influencer agencies, should have an easier time creating benchmark pricing.

So how much should clients spend? Here's my food for thought options.

Rule 1

Clients should spend 5% to 10% of revenues on marketing.

To support this spending ratio for this book, I studied the research of three advertising budget experts. Here is some support for the percentage approach.

MarketingWeek's Mark Ritson quotes economist Dr. Grace Kite:

> A "good rule of thumb" is to spend between 5% and 10% of your revenues on advertising. That proportion will usually enable you to achieve competitive excess share of voice and ensure the maximum return on investment.

CHAPTER 19

Rule 2

Aim for a share-of-voice advantage.

Bottom line… spend more than your competition. Makes sense, yes? Need support? Les Binet (group head of effectiveness, adam&eveDDB) and Peter Field reported in an IPA article that "historically, share of voice has driven share of market."

A laugh. An advertising agency tradition is to advise clients keep spending on marketing during a recession. Does this advice get taken? Maybe half the time.

Rule 3

The CPG-based 60/40 rule suggests that brands use 60% of their budget for brand building and 40% for activation.

Is this a solid, always go-to ratio? Of course not. But we need to start somewhere. Here are two perspectives:

1. Activation provokes an immediate response and sale. CMOs and CFOs like this. This is today's holy grail.

2. Brand building builds long-term sales and revenues. CMOs like this. But in difficult economic times, CMOs need to drive immediate activity.

Need support for long-term brand building versus activation?

> According to CEO Brian Chesky, 90% of Airbnb traffic happens directly, not through search. Instead, its ad spend has been used on brand campaigns that inform consumers about various services Airbnb offers. (eMarketer)

How about the brands that are well established in your head? Did you need to see a Patagonia ad to get you to buy that down vest?

Rule 4

Estimate the job via a tight work estimate and tack on your profit margin. Simply put, cost + markup = price. Work with the client to establish a detailed scope of work (SOW).

Easy? Nope. Some words from Michael Farmer the author of the appropriately named *Madison Avenue Manslaughter*. Here is a tidbit from an interview I did for my "Advertising Stories" podcast.

> I've worked with, Ogilvy, Gray, VMLY&R, BBDO, you name it. I've worked with them all. I don't know of a single holding company agency that has yet developed a methodology for measuring the amount of work they do so that they can better negotiate fees and resources with our clients.

Those are the big boys. And they have a hard time estimating.

If you're just starting out, you might need to lower your price to get a few new clients in the door. Make sure to make this pricing flexibility a short-term business-building proposition. Consider having that set-price productized service offer to get things rolling.

Hours vs. Value

I discuss financials in detail in Chapter 20, "Show Me the Money." However, one of the more difficult agency-to-client discussions is often about the relationship between the hours required to deliver a specific job and the ultimate marketplace value of the deliverable.

The value model aligns agency work with measurable client goals. This should increase client satisfaction. But establishing value is subjective and can be hard to track.

What is the real value of super brand driving advertising? What could an agency charge for sales-building brilliance? What could agencies have charged for:

CHAPTER 19

- OREO's Super Bowl blackout tweet "Power out? No problem. You can still dunk in the dark."
- The Capital One strapline "What's in your wallet?"
- Apple's Mac launch TV commercial "1984"
- Budweiser's "Whassup" or Guinness's "Guinness is good for you."
- The Always campaign: #LikeAGirl
- Tubi's 2023 Super Bowl screen-takeover commercial from Mischief

In this case, we are going well beyond the specific hours it took the agency to come up with the big idea.

This is about the true market-building value of work itself.
A sharp agency team can go from an observation to an insight to a brilliant advertising idea in a day. Should the agency charge for the eight hours (let's say four people at the blended rate of $350 per hour = $11,000) or the true value of the big idea?

Budweiser reported that supermarket sales were up 7.9% for the first four weeks of the DDB Chicago Whassup campaign versus the year-ago period, according to Information Resources Inc.

Maybe Bud gave DDB Chicago a bonus. Or a nice tip. But probably not. At least the agency won a Grand Clio. What was Bud's ultimate gift? DDB was fired in 2011.

The idea of how to attribute high value to a big creative idea has been long-term agency-to-client discussion. I've never yet seen an industry-wide solution.

What More Do Clients Really Need?

An agency can deliver all or some of the master list of client wants. However, if these deliverables are not supported by superior agency service and conscious relationship building ethos, clients will split.

It's the service, stupid.

I was trained in account management skills when I started out at

CLIENT MANAGEMENT

New York's Dancer Fitzgerald Sample. DFS had clients like P&G, HP, Nabisco, Toyota, and Sara Lee, and it understood that client touch was a critical element in maintaining ongoing relationships and setting the agency up for even more new projects from these clients.

In my first year I attended weekly management training sessions. I've used this training as I advanced at major agencies, as a company CEO, as an agency owner, and even today as a consultant. Understanding the art of people-to-people skills and communications management has propelled my career and client successes.

Sadly, most of today's ad agencies do not provide any training for their account managers or client touchers. Money is simply too tight. CEOs and COOs are too busy. Not taking the time to train your account managers is nuts.

Please, no crying. Below are some of the account management skills that are must haves and can be taught. Easily.

CHAPTER 20

CHAPTER 20

The Savvy Account Manager

The best, as in long-term client relationships, are driven by excellent service. Yes, the clients want strategic thinking, superior creative, breakthrough media planning, and efficient execution. But if the agency is not delivering superior service, the client will eventually split.

I was the client of agencies for seven years. No question that the work came first. But the relationship could easily have been eroded via poor service.

Why Clients Split

If a major cause of agency dismissal in a longer-term relationship is perceived poor service, then all agencies need to address this potential issue fast. It's imperative that agency management ask their client "How are we doing?" on a scheduled basis. Make asking this service question an element of your overall service offer.

I also recommend a more detailed annual assessment. That said, one fast path to understanding client love (or lack thereof) is to use Net Promoter Score (NPS) research. An NPS survey measures the likelihood that a client would recommend your agency to others. The client rates the agency on a scale of 1 to 10.

The Account Manager Role

Since most agencies have account managers who handle day-to-day client communications, agencies need to do a better job of training these frontline employees. This training can also be used for any client-touch person. Even self-taught one-person shops.

Is training necessary in a busy agency environment? Um, yes. Need an unfortunate 13% kick in the ass? Here's a *wow!* as reported in the 2022 *What Clients Think* report from the UK's Up in the Light.

> Only 13% of clients stated that their agency "regularly exceeds their expectations."

Thirteen percent. I'm sure you are saying not *my* agency. How do you know this? Have you asked lately?

The Kick-Ass Account Manager

To get a handle on how well agencies describe the account manager role, I looked at account manager job postings from two established agencies. Here's a quick look at how two agencies talk about the account manager role in their Career website sections.

WPP Sydney senior account manager position:

> Key Responsibilities: Build an open, honest, and trusting relationship with the client, the account management team,

creative department, and all other agency partners.
1. Actively contribute to the agency's culture.
2. Work with the Senior AD on leading the brand and BTL strategy and how it connects to creative.
3. Create the best possible opportunities for creative development, by supporting teams in creative development and understanding how it delivers to business challenges.
4. Work alongside a village team with like-minded colleagues, ensuring that teamwork and collaboration are front and center of that process.
5. Be involved in team development and support your team environment through collaboration and inclusivity.

Goodby Silverstein & Partners senior account director position:

For us a great Senior Account Director does the following things really well:
1. Clearly defines the client's business problem and gets people in the Agency excited to work on it.
2. Provides their own point-of-view that is considerate of both the Client's and Agency's viewpoints, but not necessarily beholden to either one of them.
3. Serves the needs of the individuals on their team and on the account.
4. Constantly set (and if necessary, change) the conditions on the account to allow people to do their best work.

Wow is all I can say after reading these job descriptions. Account management is a complex role that requires the ability to dig into the client's objectives; savvy communications skills; being up to date on new technologies, strategic, and marketing insights; reflects agency culture; and understands how to motivate agency teams.

Agencies often hope that account managers somehow learn how to deliver these services via osmosis. Not good enough.

Account Management Training

Why not have an account management training program? Training your staff in account management skills delivers a range of benefits. An account management program doesn't have to be complex, time consuming, or expensive.

In addition to ensuring that agency employees know how to deliver superior service, gauge client satisfaction, and are up to date on industry trends, training (upskilling) has additional benefits directly related to agency-wide employee satisfaction.

1. Training drives higher employee morale
2. It fosters company loyalty and instills corporate culture
3. It increases staff retention
4. It is a positive recruitment tool

Here is a radical idea. You could even invite clients to your training program. Show them how important the delivery of service is to your company. Ask for their input.

Here's my 12-point advice for agency leadership on how to build (and motivate) an exceptional account manager.

Training can be done in brief bite-sized sessions.

1. Define what a spectacular client relationship looks like. Have stated relationship objectives.
2. Make continuous learning a part of agency culture. Curate a set of tools and resources, including articles, group Zoom education meetings, and YouTube videos—even relevant YouTube quickies—that will help train your account managers on how

to manage clients.

    An ongoing training program will make sure that account managers are up to speed on the latest advertising trends and are a step or two ahead of the clients. This program will also foster interdepartmental communication.

3. Account managers need to know the details of their account's P&L. Train the manager on how to help manage their costs and profit margin. Get way ahead of any profit problems before they fester. The account manager, not the busy CFO, is on the front line.
4. Create a system for scope-of-work management. A scope-of-work agreement defines the work the agency is going to do for the client and the time it will spend on the work. It includes a definition of deliverables, the timeline, agency and client responsibilities, and reports. The account manager should work closely with the project management team to ensure that the job is on time and meets client expectations and to help avoid scope creep.

    Managing evil scope creep, and related (often difficult) client communications, is not easy. It requires both real-time agency systems and the art of client handling. I was brought up being called an account executive. I was a bit surprised to find out that UK agencies called their account executives account handlers—a rather direct way to define the job. Train your account people in the art of client handling. Gentle handling.
5. Help account executives understand that listening closely to the client's objectives, as in really listening, is critically important in building a trusted relationship.

    Go further and train the team on what is called active listening, which is defined by the Center for Creative Leadership as follows:

Active listening requires you to listen attentively to a speaker, understand what they're saying, respond and reflect on what's being said, and retain the information for later. This keeps both listener and speaker actively engaged in the conversation.

A key attribute of Active Listening is leaning in. Body language works to help make clients think you're listening. Leaning in even works on telephone or Zoom calls. Have a Zoom or Google Meet best practices POV.

6. Make sure account managers know how to anticipate client needs and issues. Think developing a client-radar mindset.

    Shep Hykin, a customer service expert, calls this anticipatory customer service. A brilliant example comes from the '70s and '80s TV show M*A*S*H.

One of the characters, Corporal Walter "Radar" O'Reilly, played by Gary Burghoff, set a standard for customer service. He worked for Colonel Potter, who ran the unit. It was always a good laugh when Colonel Potter barked out a request for a file and Radar was walking into his office with the file before the Colonel even finished his request. It was as if he could read minds, or as his nickname indicates, as if he had radar.

Understanding the client, like really well, will help your account people to be able to be a step ahead of client needs. There is nothing as powerful as being able to answer a question before it is asked.

    Building the art of curiosity is important. The goal is to anticipate client needs and let the client know that y'all are ahead of the curve.

7. Account managers need to take the time to learn about the agency's successes, history and culture, branding, and best client case histories. Manger 1 might not know the details of a successful program delivered last year by Manger 2. Have a system for sharing experiences across accounts.

8. Clients need and want strategic guidance. Have a schedule for sending them the agency's thought leadership materials and relevant information about their programs, competitors, and industries. You want to look and act like a valuable strategic leader.

    Consider providing account managers with a templated approach to thought leadership distribution. Offer a micro-training program to cover the basics of thought leadership development and distribution options.

9. Teach presentation skills: Giving a persuasive presentation comes naturally to some but not all. Presentation skills can be taught. Start inside the agency. These skills are particularly important these days as we are doing more virtual presentations.

    Have an agency approach to how to run and manage an online presentation. This includes branding, backgrounds, lighting, and sound. Buy your remote staff the right equipment.

    Prospective clients often ask that the people who will be working on their account be in the initial pitch meeting. Don't wait until the day before a pitch to teach your pitch crew stellar presentations skills.

    In fact, why not take everyone in the agency through a couple of recent pitches?

10. Management skills, as in knowing how to manage in-house communications and how to share client objectives and strategies, can be taught. Being conscious of how to start and control agency jobs and to be efficient is a must-have skill.

    How to delegate, coach, support, and direct across the agency are not necessarily native skills. A bit of training will help.

    Support agency and client communications with a set of shell documents, including your project scope proposals, creative brief, contact reports, and best practices on how to use communication tools like email and Slack.

11. Account managers have a personal brand. Look at how your key

players look to the outside world. I know savvy clients look at everyone's LinkedIn page. Even Facebook and Instagram pages. No, I'm not asking you to be a personal brand policeman. Just help your folks understand that the agency brand includes the power of their very own brand.

My takeaway here is that agency leadership should not leave client relationships to chance and that even a fast-paced training program could reduce client turnover and, better yet, increase client love.

This program could be run beyond account management as many people in the agency occasionally touch the clients. Manage those touches.

CHAPTER 21

Show Me the Money

Savvy Accounting

I mentioned at the start of this book that my Oregon agency didn't have a set-in-stone business plan. We should have. But nope. What we did have was a solid approach to tracking our financials.

Our agency financials were tracked by our CFO, and she was supported by scheduled reviews with our accountant.

We had monthly internal profit analysis reports that were designed to quickly provide a look at agency profitability and productivity. Our profit analysis report included the following:

1. **Gross margin analysis**
   The objective was to increase account by account efficiency and to locate any red flags before they caught on fire.
2. **Overhead analysis**
   We continually reviewed overhead line items including rent,

staff costs, insurance (corporate and health), and technology costs.

3. **Free cash flow analysis**

   As an agency owner, our quarterly free cash flow calculation either made me sleep like a baby or become an insomniac. We calculated our free cash flow by subtracting capital expenditures from net cash.

4. **Labor costs assessment**

   We had a goal of allocating approximately 50% of revenue to salaries and benefits.

5. **Staff utilization**

   The staff accurately tracked their time, and these reports allowed us to create utilization rates that compared billable hours to total hours worked. Our utilization rate helped us calculate hourly rates. This information also helped us to determine future hiring needs and any potential skill set and service mix deficits.

6. **Account receivables**

   My CFO was a genius in tracking and managing accounts receivable. The genius part came in as a focused approach to invoicing and examination of any overdue payments. Her job included working with me on all proposals and client billing agreements. The genius also came in as she established close working relationships with our clients' accounting departments to ensure that we were paid on time.

Your Agency: A Bottom-Line Model From AMI

Getting back to "Keep it simple, stupid!"

I am a big fan of Drew McClellan's AMI (Agency Management Institute). Drew advises his agency clients to observe what he calls the 55-25-20 rule.

Spend 55% of your AGI (adjusted gross income, or

gross billings minus cost of goods) on salaries and benefits and 25% on overhead and drive 20% to the bottom line.

Back To How to Price

"My company needs a 12-month marketing program for our DTC Amazon store. I'd like a proposal please."

"I need to rebrand my international pet food brand."

We all like to hear these lovely words. What marketing services provider wouldn't? The prospective client's question means that your agency optimized its business development program, got the attention of a prospective client, killed the RFP, had a sales meeting where you sounded smart and experienced, and now the client is interested in getting a solid proposal.

The next step is to price out the services they need, or think they need. How do you get to that magic number? You are now about to estimate the job via determining the value of your expertise plus staff time plus overhead plus experience plus your profit margin goal. Getting there can be rather complicated.

1. Does the client have clear business objectives and KPIs? Have you discussed their rationale? Be their Sherpa, not just an order taker.
2. Is the client an experienced marketer? Have they done a program like this before?
3. Does the client have a stated budget? How did they arrive at that? Will they provide you with what they have spent in the past?
4. Do you have predetermined pricing models so that every job does not have to priced à la carte?

Just for laughs I searched on Google for "advertising agency pricing models" and it delivered 613 million results (on another day it was 719 million), so you ad folks (and clients of course) appear to be working hard on establishing agency pricing models.

I'm about to state the obvious. Getting your pricing scenario and system right will result in higher profits, less agency stress, and even a happier client. You want to get paid fairly and reduce client relationship tension points and get past any future surprises.

First a bit of history.

The word *agency* comes from the time when agencies acted as sales agents for newspapers. If the agency brought business to the newspaper, the newspaper paid them a 15% commission. This evolved to the agencies providing creative and media services. The good old days.

My client Johnson & Johnson had a $75 million media budget. The agency charged the 15% fee that delivered $11.25 million to the agency. We also charged 16.5% for production. Believe me, our margins were high.

The 15% fee started to shrink in the 1990s when clients figured out that they could reduce this percentage and still receive the required service. Or so they thought. Agencies had little choice but to go along. Those good old days disappeared.

Today, agency pricing is all over the map.

5 Pricing Models

There are five main pricing models. I'm sure that some creative CFOs have other thoughts.

1. Hourly rates

You charge a client for staff time by the hour. Generally, an agency charges using a single blended rate. The blended rate is calculated by taking the average hourly rate of all employees that will work on the job and then multiplying by the number of hours it will take to complete the project.

In this case it is critical that you use some form of time sheets which will never be totally accurate. Yet, having them is a must.

What do agencies charge? I'll include this example as background. According to Credo's 2022 digital marketing industry pricing survey, on average, US-based digital marketing firms charge from $148 per hour for SEO and $152 per hour for PPC work. This is lower than the $200 per hour average that my average ad agency client charges.

The pros are that you get paid for the hours you work. The downside is that the client usually needs a fixed cost and the hourly rate can cause friction when the job is affected by scope creep and when a client questions each billable item.

2. Fixed rate

Clients like fixed project rates. The agency calculates the rate by estimating the numbers of hours it will take to complete the project, multiplying that by the agency's hourly blended rate, and then adding in the agency's margin goal.

A way to manage the fixed rate is to have one or more agency benchmark rates to see if estimates fall inside of the range of average ad agency rates. The benchmark rate is calculated by looking at average industry rates based on region, size of the company, and a few other data points, including agency pricing history.

The pros are that this should be an easy discussion. However, the agency must manage scope creep, which can become a serious agency profitably issue.

3. Performance or value pricing

That value thing, again. In this case, you get paid for delivering performance value based on measurable results. This can be hard to calculate if the agency is providing multiple services.

Back to the predigital era. While we wanted to get paid for success, the array of marketing factors limited the ability to point to any one agency deliverable's effectiveness. I recall conversations with clients about performance pricing where performance was also affected by the creative messaging, media spend, product distribution, product promotions, and the efficacy of the product or service itself. Mucho factors that could make or break a clear path to understanding what drove performance.

Some good news. In the digital world an agency can establish digital conversion metrics and the value of each conversion.

A pro is that the value proposition helps the client and agency be aligned behind a definition of success. Most of the time.

4. Retainer

A retainer is an agreement between the agency and client that sets a rate and timetable for a project or ongoing program. Goals are defined in an onboarding session and the work is scoped out. The agency works closely with the client to determine what work will need to be completed and the timetable, and then agree on a monthly number of hours to meet the objectives.

Both parties benefit from pricing clarity and a predetermined payment system.

Considerations

It can be difficult to agree to a retainer with a new client you've never worked with. Can they stay the course?

Some clients will find it difficult to commit to a retainer if they don't have a way to judge the work or success.

It can be difficult to fire a bad actor client when in a retainer partnership.

That said, agencies sure like knowing what revenues, and profits, can be preplanned.

5. Consulting

Consulting is the delivery of strategic advice designed to reach, engage, and convert customers.

Consulting includes client and industry market research, competitive analysis, and marketing and advertising recommendations that can lead to a long-term relationship.

Many agencies would like to have the pricing power of a McKinsey Digital. You can set this up over time. Get known as a strategist and make this a standalone offer. Start with your brilliant though leadership.

Cost Management

"Only the paranoid survive." This rather important message was delivered by Intel founder Andy Grove's 1999 mega bestseller of the same name.

As we all know, shit happens. Be prepared. Always be paranoid (ABP), a close cousin of always be closing (ABC).

We can't really plan on clients staying forever or maintaining their spend, we can't predict macroeconomic events or what's on the minds of Putin and Xi, and we can't control our award-winning creative director going to start their own agency with our largest client.

External shit will happen. The only element of your agency business that you have *total* control of is your cost of doing business.

Understand your cash runway. We're seeing many well-funded, yet low-revenue Silicon Valley startups run out of cash. Your agency is not immune. If you think you're on a serious path toward doom, just close your doors or begin to plan on how to merge or sell.

Reinvent your business plan (maybe your business itself). Never let a good crisis go to waste. Look at your existing business plan. Consider tossing it. What plan, and advertising agency structure, makes sense today and for the future?

Think about what a client would buy from you in a recessionary environment, not what you want to sell.

Back to paranoia and the need for being nimble. "If you don't like change, you're going to like irrelevance even less." A bit of guidance from US Army general Eric Shinseki.

Dial up that scenario planning. Think through three or four business scenarios. What would you do if a quarter or half of your clients reduce

CHAPTER 21

their marketing? What growing industry categories or new media should you begin to specialize in? Get into future think. Why not offer scenario planning to your clients? Include a market review, some future think, and recommendations. I bet McKinsey Digital does this.

A hard truth: Since staff costs account for at least 50% of your cost structure, you need to examine staff performance—often. Be realistic.

Fire underutilized or poorly performing employees quickly. Harsh? You bet. Occasionally I waited too long. If you know you must let some staff go, do it quickly. You want to reduce any internal stress if you can. Don't leave employees guessing or wondering why that low-energy person (today's quiet quitter) is still around.

CHAPTER 22
The Business Development Budget

A Sad Biz Dev Story

The cost and effectiveness of agency business development can make or break an agency. Let me give you a real-world worst-case example.

A Pacific Northwest agency was one of a set of digital agencies trying to land a major account. The client's pitch team wanted to see each agency's strategic approach. To win, the Northwest agency built a comprehensive plan that included custom market research and leased MarTech technology. The pitch dragged on forever and the agency was racking up staff and hard costs.

Good news: The agency won the account.

Bad news: The pitch became so expensive that the agency almost went out of business *after* winning the account. The agency's costs included the cost of the initial RFP response and a four-month pitch that included spec work. Add in the agency's work for this new client plus the client's

90-day payment schedule. The cost of the RFP response, managing and crafting the pitch itself (mega labor hours), and the actual work, once won, had the agency essentially working for free for more than six months.

Could the agency have managed down this insane scenario? Not sure. Every pitch and client engagement is by nature unique. That said, the agency could have had a better handle on what was coming when they initially interviewed the client. However, I'm not sure that the client was forthcoming or really knew what they needed in the first place. Unfortunately, many clients are not skilled at running a pitch.

The takeaway is that agencies shouldn't pitch everything. Period. Spend the time to understand the client's needs, motivations, and past agency history and know why you should be the winner and what the search and pitch details are—including payment terms (yes, often hard to gauge). But if anything doesn't feel right or professional, then bail.

Always keep in mind the cost of pitching and that, at best, an agency will win only 30% of the time.

Budgeting for Business Development

Determining the balance between the cost of business development and its effect on agency profitability is not easy. Having an established business development plan and annual budget is essential to managing down business development costs and driving up the win rate.

Business development costs include:
- Agency management costs. As an agency CEO I allocated 50% of my time to business development. I view 50% as a goal for most agency CEOs or COOs. It helped that I viewed biz dev as fun.
- Internal staff costs. This includes anyone who touches the business development plan plus the salary and commission plan of a business development manager.
- Annual marketing costs. These include thought leadership develop-

ment and any expenditures related to ABM, SEM, agency advertising, and other marketing systems or platforms. Your business development plan should include cost estimates.
- Out of pocket costs. Think freelancers, developers, and software purchases.
- Onerous payment terms. Payment terms have evolved into insanity and even bullying. The 2022 Keurig Dr Pepper PR agency search included the marketer's request for 360-day payment terms, meaning the winning firm would not get its full payment for nearly a year. Try telling your dry cleaner that you will pay your bill in 360 days.

Do Not Pitch That Account

My book *The Levitan Pitch. Buy This Book. Win More Pitches* spends a fair amount of time discussing the bottom-line pain and people burnout issues related to the cost of pitching—especially pitching too often. A big problem is an agency not having tight selection criteria for the type of accounts the agency should pitch.

It's difficult for an agency to say no to a desirable client looking for a new agency. It's way less difficult if an agency has a specialization, an expertise. Expertise will help you know what accounts to go after and, importantly, which accounts should hire you. Think of having that expertise that helps you say no, this account is not in my wheelhouse.

Here's my topline take on larger-account pitch management. With full-on pitches costing thousands in bucks and time, agencies should have a go-or-no-go system to assess the potential of every pitch.

Reggie Jackson, an ex–New York Yankee, is a baseball hall of famer. He got in with a .261 batting average. That's only 3 hits for every 10 times at bat. In agency think, this would mean that the agency would be Hall of Fame material if they won 3 out of every 10 pitches.

Let's do some larger agency math using the 1:3 ratio.

Based on my personal experience, conversations with agency CEOs, and a review of existing data, on average, small to medium agencies respond to 10 RFPs and participate in six pitches per year. Your mileage may vary, but let's go with this.

My estimated cost per a larger agency RFP is $15,000 based on 150 hours of work at a direct labor cost of $100 per hour. At 10 RFPs per year, that's a participation cost of $150,000 per year.

A conservative estimate of an average finalist pitch—which includes external and internal meetings, pitch management, strategic planning, writing, creative work, pitch design (as in leave-behinds and supporting digital programs), the pitch itself, travel and expenses, and post-presentation follow-up costs—is approximately $35,000. If an agency does six pitches per year, that's $210,000.

Obviously, given the size range between multinational networks and small shops these numbers seem fair for the average agency, and they help frame the issue.

Using my scenario, the total annual cost for RFPs and pitching comes to $360,000. This number doesn't include the day-to-day costs of business development. If you add in management, creative, analog and digital marketing, and business development director time, an agency could easily top out at over $500,000 in labor and outsourced business development costs per year. I am ball-parking here just to get to a reference number.

A total of $500,000 means that you better have a solid business development plan and budget and sound who-should-we-pitch criteria.

Smaller agencies and one-person shops have to recognize that the time to pitch takes away for getting the actual client work done. This cost can be huge.

The Resources section includes a go–no go, to-pitch-or-not-to-pitch assessment tool.

Do a Client Assessment

Here's another angle to help you decide which accounts to pitch. As an agency owner, I always cherished four client attributes. Frankly, if I could get just two of these, I'd be happy. Our agency-of-record client Nike delivered all four.

1. Fame. Famous clients look great on your client roster, act as poster children for prospective clients that need third-party reassurance that you deliver results, and help you woo more talented employees. Having famous clients will make your parents proud.
2. Creative love. You are in the creative services industry because you are creative and want clients who respect creativity. Creativity to me extends beyond just the creative idea into creative media, strategic thinking, market insights, and technology. That said, the bottom line for most agencies is that we want to make great advertising programs, and to get there, you need clients who want that too.
3. Cash. Fame is nice. Clio Awards are nice. But cash rules. After all, you are in business. In this case, money means having clients that deliver agency profits. No profits means no staff, no creative, no brilliant social media strategies, no awards to win—and no agency.
4. Niceness. Early in my career, I was given the advice that I should only work with clients who align with my agency's values and share mutual respect. To take it a step further, work with nice people who you like. If I appear to have gone all gooey, I listened, and it was great advice. Life is too short to work with assholes.

Nice is a good thing in a business where having fun is a key benefit.

CHAPTER 23

CHAPTER 23

The Business Development Director

74% Failure Rate Blues

Ah, the agency business development director. Agencies like to call this position's responsibility business development rather than sales because… well, because business development can sound less salesy to our sensitive agency ears. But it is sales after all.

Whatever you call it, I'm not sure there's a more difficult job inside an agency than that of business development director.

The tenure of a new business director is now two years or less. In a survey conducted by RSW/US, only 26% of new business directors were considered successful. Turn that around. That's a 74% failure rate.

CHAPTER 23

What Can We Do?

First, let's all agree that even the best business development director cannot sell an advertising agency that doesn't have clear marketing goals, a reasonable sales budget, a distinctive and competitive positioning (please!), services that at least look undeniably effective to the outside world, IP, and committed and active agency management.

Everyone at the agency must understand that even your favorite clients will eventually walk out the back door and must be replaced via an active 24/7 business development plan—in other words, fill the pipeline. Therefore, business development programs must be treated with the same respect and attention to detail that the agency delivers to its clients.

Make sure you have a strong competitive message and story. Always ask the question, If you were a client, would you hire you? If not, figure out why. Fast.

To get the job done, run business development with the same attention and systems that you deliver to clients.

Four Issues That Help Business Development Directors Fail

1. Little management patience. All too often the business development director isn't given the time to build out the plan and tactics before all those new expected clients start to roll in. If the average tenure of a business development director is around two years, it means a lot of these folks are being hired (and let go) way too soon in the sales cycle to make a sales dent. Worse, agency management doesn't understand the sales process itself. Maybe the boss should take a bit of sales training.
2. A stranger in a strange land. Today's wonderful business development director often comes from outside the agency and might have to live with the impersonal business constraints of working

from home.

Distance is not a good thing. Business development managers need to really understand the deep workings of the agency. How you do this long distance requires the care and attention of agency management.

What happens when the new business development director has little chance to integrate into the distributed agency and experience its culture? This is a serious issue. It is incumbent on agency management to integrate this important new hire into the organization. Have an onboarding plan before they arrive. It starts with intelligent onboarding and must include an alignment between the business development director and clearly stated agency sales objectives.

3. Compensation. Another reason business development directors fail is that the agency does not have a sound, sales-oriented compensation plan that reflects the objectives of the master business development program.

Incentives baked into the compensation plan must be designed to meet agency objectives. Sounds reasonable. But most agencies don't have sales experience and don't know how to write a strategic incentive-based comp plan. Elements should include:
- A decent, livable base salary
- A bonus when the business development manager delivers a meeting with a key prospect that is on your must-meet ABM list. Virtually every agency leader tells me that they can close the deal once they have a one-on-one conversation with that prospective client. Reward that business development director for getting you in that room
- Payout of an incentive-inducing percentage of the first year's revenues (not profits, because an agency's profit ratio is not the responsibility of the business development director).

4. Focus. Do not have the director manage any new accounts. This would be a major distraction. A big-time understatement.

CHAPTER 23

5. Business development is an agencywide responsibility that needs to be supported across agency functions. No new clients, no raises.

A 4A's report cited that 90% of agency staff say they must figure things out on their own due to the lack of training. I recommend that all business development activists—anyone who plays a role in agency marketing—are offered some form of basic sales training.

I put a sample business development director contract in the Resources section.

CHAPTER 24

How to Build, Buy, and Sell an Agency

According to US Census data, the US advertising and public relations industry reached an aggregated revenue of roughly $154 billion in 2021. It was $81 billion in 2011.

There is money in them darn advertising hills. To get at it, you could start from scratch, buy an existing agency, or sell out for massive bucks.

Build Your New Agency

New advertising and digital agencies are started every day. IBISWorld reports that there are now 87,712 agencies. There were 60,000 in 2012. US annualized advertising agency growth is +4.8%. Why?

1. New marketing platforms need new agencies. There were no TikTok or influencer agencies a few years ago. A range of AI

CHAPTER 24

specialists is coming.
2. The major consultancies are playing at advertising and have launched their own well-funded creative agencies. Accenture Interactive bought Droga5.
3. Older evolving platforms like SEO need new blood and ideas.
4. Hot teams leave their current agency, often with a client, to become their own boss.
5. A 25-year-old just might just go digital nomad and break out of the corporate world of an Omnicom. Go nomad in Chiang Mai. Sounds good to me.
6. Starting that new agency from your local coffee shop carries a rather low cost of entry.

I've covered the major tools you'll need to run a successful agency. Here's a quick recap.
1. Write that business plan. Know how and from who you'll you make bucks.
2. Define your brand positioning and expertise.
3. Build that thought leadership plan.
4. Determine staffing requirements, including full-time employees, freelancers, and how to manage a distributed workforce. Hire slowly.
5. Set your pricing models and systemized processes.
6. Understand your cost structure. From IBIS:
   The highest costs for business in the advertising agencies industry in the US as a percentage of revenue are Wages (31.1%), Purchases (7.6%), and Rent & Utilities (6.6%).
7. Build out a business development plan and tools including a sales-oriented website. Make being unignorable an objective. Manage workload by employing the art of "Keep it simple, stupid!"
8. Do the legal and financial work to understand and plan your financial goals and guidelines.

That's the tough stuff. Time consuming. But you want to hit the ground running. Deal with the detail upfront.

Now for some fun. Every advertising agency I've ever met has gone through the agony and ecstasy of naming their company.

The Agency Name Game

Other than the positioning gyrations all agencies must go through, what services to concentrate on, the design and redesign of their website, and so on, how they name themselves is one of their most important branding decisions.

I worked for three advertising agencies. Two were founder named agencies: Dancer Fitzgerald Sample (New York's largest agency; remember "Where's the beef?") and Saatchi & Saatchi Advertising Worldwide. The third was my very own Portland agency with its current usage name Citrus.

Do advertising names matter? Wow, this is a tough one to answer. As you'll see from the different naming conventions listed below, how one chooses a name is a journey.

Once again, some thoughts from Al Reis's *The 22 Immutable Laws of Marketing*. Al on one of the great advertising taglines and names:

> "With a name like Smucker's, it has to be good." Most companies, especially family companies, would never make fun of their own name. Yet the Smucker family did, which is one reason why Smucker's is the No. 1 brand of jams and jellies. If your name is bad, you have two choices: change the name or make fun of it.

Smucker's hard-to-ignore name helped it become a leader in the preserves market. Can you name any other brands in the preserves market? More names you ask. Just for the hell of it, here are some of the names from *Ad Age*'s 2022 Small Agency Awards:

- Mojo Supermarket
- Movers+Shakers
- Fred & Fared
- Quality Meats
- Preacher
- Alto
- Opinionated
- NVE Experiential
- Media Matters
- Zulu Alpha Kilo

Do any of these agency names instill immediate confidence? A must-call reaction? Stand out from the crowd? Communicate a benefit? Man, tough questions to answer. However, these are all better than the insanely unmemorable VML&R. This name deserves a WTF!

My current favorite is Movers+Shakers. This brand name has energy and kind of meets the client pain point of finding a way to live through an era of disruption.

The drill is that names do matter. Spend the time to think through the naming process.

Five Types of Brand Names

1. Neologisms

A neologism, or new word, is just what you would expect it to be: a word that is created.

Pros: New inventive products can make the new name synonymous with their product (Xerox, Kleenex, Microsoft, eTrade). They are distinctive and are globally friendly. There are no legal or copyright issues. Neologisms are an easy domain name get.

Cons: Neologisms have no meaning and initially take more marketing energy to become recognized.

Agency example: Smak calls itself the "impact agency."

2. Current usage words

Words that already have meaning. Brands with current usage names include Oracle, Sprint, Apple, Tide, and Fidelity.

Pros: Current usage names telegraph brand values (Apple is friendly), tap the name's inherent attributes (Sprint is fast), can quickly trigger positive imagery (Tide is fresh and clean), and communicate service messages with less marketing spending (Uber).

Cons: Marketers must make sure that current usage names accurately reflect the brand's image and do not raise a negative or confusing response. There may be trademark and domain hurdles.

Agency example: Opinionated. They say, "Opinionated people make opinionated work, and given the dumpster-fire state of media these days, that's the only kind of work that gets noticed."

3. Hybrids

Hybrids combine current usage names. You might be typing on a ThinkPad laptop. Or brushed your teeth with Aquafresh. I just played games on my PlayStation.

Pros: Hybrids are like current usage names in that they quickly communicate a brand message. In addition, the combination can build on the power of the two-word combination. Finally, hybrids reduce the issues associated with copyrighting the name.

Cons: The cons are like those of current usage names. The two words could cause a bit of confusion.

Agency example: Media.Monks is a sweet name for a media agency. I want the expertise, concentration, and dedication of a monk.

4. Acronyms

Acronyms are letter combinations that generally reflect a multiple word name. In many cases, the Acronym has taken the place of the original name (IBM was once called International Business Machines).

Pros: Acronyms can be distinctive and have few legal issues.

Cons: Acronyms require marketing to make them memorable. They have little inherent meaning, and since they essentially say nothing about the brand, they add little value to the customer branding experience. They can also be hard to remember.

An easy agency target that I must mention again: Who the heck came up with the ridiculous and impossible to remember agency name VMLY&R?

5. Founder names
Founder-based names abound across many service and product categories. Ford, Chase, Jensen, and Schwab all are names of company founders.

Pros: Using the founder's name adds direct personal credibility. It helps if the founder has built, or is willing to build, an authoritative personal brand.

Cons: In most cases using a founder name requires marketing to seed the name. It helps if the founder has a strong personal brand. Think Vaynerchuck.

Agency examples: Allison+Partners is, guess what, named after Scott Allison. Can you name the team that runs the brand and design firm Antonio & Paris?

The Naming Process

Yes, there is a strategic process to naming. Selecting a name should be an important element of your brand-new advertising agency's marketing plan. A new name also works for agencies that need a facelift and repositioning.

I bought Oregon's Ralston Group (a founder name), and then moved to Ralston360 when we added social media to our mix, and then to Citrus when we bought the design firm Citrus. A better name all around.

Things to Consider
You cannot begin to name your brand without establishing clear brand positioning and business objectives, which in the case of ad agencies

sometimes just means sounding cool. Little Hands of Stone is arguably kinda cool and is certainly distinctive. And the strange name makes me wonder just who these guys are. HawkSEM is an expert SEM agency.

Craft your agency's story and personality. Are your smart, friendly, quirky, sincere, a quant jock, strategic, or just give good lunch? Before I sold my Citrus agency, I thought of renaming it PORTLAND to leverage the city's creative reputation. I mentioned London's agency LONDON Advertising. Both London and Portland are well known for their creativity. Hello, AUSTIN.

Do a competitive review. OK, this is a duh. A competitive review should examine your competitors' brand positionings and brand names. Depending on who you talk to, there are like 4,000 agencies in the USA. Sounding like the competition won't help you stand out.

A Name Story

Here's a little competitive-name happy-ending story for you. I sold Citrus the agency in 2014. A couple of weeks after the deal closed, a sale where the name Citrus was dissolved by the new owner, I was sitting in my room in LA's the Standard Hotel and checked my voice mail. An unknown lawyer said I must call him immediately about a VERY serious company issue. He was being rather aggressive. So, I gave him a call.

No polite chit chat, the tough a–hole lawyer dives into a threatening diatribe about how I must get rid of the name Citrus because his agency client, another Citrus, wants us gone. If I don't do as he says, he will sue the shit out of me.

While the dude is doing his nasty lawyer thing, I'm thinking this conversation should be fun. So, I play along and let the guy rant and rave and tell me that I must change the name of my 10-year-old agency like tomorrow. I'm acting a bit nervous, but I'm telling him I can't do much. He's asking why I can't do much. After a few minutes of playful obfuscation, I say, "OK, you win. I'll change the name." And I hang up. I never mentioned that my own Citrus agency was no longer alive.

CHAPTER 24

I use this story to tell you to do a research dive before you launch.

Brand Name Development

Once you have your positioning and a deep understanding of your competition, it's time to review the types of names that will work hard for you.

1. Are these neologisms, current usage words, hybrids, acronyms, or founder names?
2. Are there application factors that must be explored? Think about how the name works in business development marketing, pronunciation, spelling issues, and new geo markets, even global applications. Future think is important.
3. Do a trademark review. A trademark review should be conducted early rather than later. Don't fall in love with an agency name you can't own (unless you have Apple-sized cojones).
4. The domain name. Ah, the URL. Ever spend hours on GoDaddy searching for usable URLs? No matter your name, be prepared to wind up with a hybrid or abbreviated URL or a unique top-level domain like .agency, .io, or .media. Today, a URL is not as important as it used to be.
5. Be Google friendly. Common usage agency names like Walrus, Basic, Naked, North, Steak, and Farm, even if you can get them, do not make for easy Google searches. And they might be gone on Twitter, Pinterest, Instagram, TikTok, and on and on.
6. Do research. Names can be tested via qualitative (ask your client friends for their opinions) or quantitative techniques, including online surveys on LinkedIn. Research? Really? It sounds a bit pedantic, right? It didn't to Paul Malmstrom of the compelling agency Mother.

"The name 'Mother' basically came out of a focus group in the general public," co-founder Paul Malmstrom told AdFreak. "Sixteen different tests were done around a randomly generated set of words, and all groups (except one) settled for 'Mother' as a top contender. The tests showed 'Mother' had pretty positive associations, ranging from 'Nurturing,' 'Familiar' to 'Don't eat with your mouth open.' To the founders this seemed to be great values to base the agency on. Words not rated as high were, for example, 'Wallet,' 'Meager' and 'Clogs,' but a close runner-up was (inexplicably) the word 'Wienerschnitzel.'"

I like the letter *A*. Way back in 2000 I founded the intelligent bot company ActiveBuddy. Check out our startup launch video on my YouTube channel. The name came from our entry into the instant messaging category with a service that let people use natural language to talk to computers. The name made sense—remember how active your IM buddy list was? Did we do massive research funded by our VCs? No, my cofounder's wife came up with the name over dinner.

That said, I witnessed a great extra benefit of the name ActiveBuddy when I attended internet industry conference and trade shows and realized we were always at the top of the attendee, exhibitor, or speaker list. Our name started with an A. While this realization was a duh moment, it made me fully understand the power of the name AAA Plumbing within the context of directories and how important it is to pay attention to every possible issue and opportunity.

Do I take my own advice? When I launched my advertising agency consultancy I went with a founder's name: Peter Levitan & Co. I thought of using SEO and Google-friendly keywords like combinations of advertising, agency, ad, business development, new business, positioning, sales, pitching, presentations... but I figured why not grow my own founder brand, my personal brand. Plus, my mommy and daddy named me.

CHAPTER 24

Buy An Agency

Existing advertising, digital, PR agencies, digital agencies get bought. It's the fastest way to grow (in size and revenues) and to acquire new marketable skills, an expanded client list, fresh talent, a new geography, and revenues.

I lived through the era of major agency acquisitions. Holding companies bought up stand-alone agencies to add geographic reach and new skill sets. Today, management consultancies acquire creative agencies to be able to deliver more fully integrated services.

Today, experts get bought faster. Brainlabs bought the influencer agency Fanbytes in 2022. Fanbytes, launched only five years earlier, works with blue-chip clients including Samsung, Nike, Ubisoft, Mattel, Estée Lauder, and H&M. It has data set of over 3 million influencers. Fanbytes is an expert. According to Market Research Future's latest report, the influencer market is expected to expand at a compound annual growth rate of 8.2% to reach $2.85 billion by 2025.

OK, this purchase is a no-brainer for Brainlabs. They got a leading influencer marketer, a set of new clients, and super smart people.

Need another expert agency purchase no-brainer? Acquisition-oriented Accenture bought The Stable. Why? The acquisition immediately led Accenture into the into the ecommerce space, omnichannel retail, direct-to-consumer (DTC) commerce and big-name clients.

My point? You'll get bought if you own something special. Yes, a duh.

Sell Your Agency

Marketing agencies get sold for various reasons. A critical element in creating a positive sales process for the sale of your agency is to know (really know) why you want to sell. Does this sound simplistic? Believe me, it isn't.

Allow me to briefly discuss the objectives and a bit of the history of my three agency buy-and-sell deals.

I'm including some personal background, as sales are personal.

Deal 1: 2002

This agency purchase deal had multiple objectives. I wanted to leverage my deep advertising and digital skills and buy a successful creative advertising agency and move out of the New York area to much greener, mellower pastures. The deal I was looking for would need to meet both business and personal needs.

I bought the Bend, Oregon, advertising agency Ralston Group. It helped that a large ski mountain was 20 minutes up the road.

Deal 2: 2006

This deal had one objective: agency growth.

My Ralston360 partner and I had been looking for over a year to buy a complementary West Coast agency in Portland, Seattle, or San Francisco. We knew we needed a foothold in a larger West Coast market to accelerate growth.

We had come up short until we found Citrus, a small Portland design firm that had an exceptionally strong relationship with Nike. We made a three-year earnout deal with the two owners and picked up two Nike agency-of-record account responsibilities: Major League Baseball and college sports. Oh, we also took the name Citrus.

We got Nike, sports marketing expertise, two smart people, decent revenues, an office in Portland, and a new name. That was a good business deal.

Deal 3: 2011

This deal had two objectives: It was time for me to move on, and I wanted to keep my agency intact for the benefit of my staff and clients.

By the ninth year of owning and running Citrus, I was starting to burnout I had put in my sixteen years at Saatchi & Saatchi Advertising

CHAPTER 24

Worldwide's New York and London offices, I had been CEO of two internet startups, and I had grown Citrus and its national client base, including Nike, Dr. Martens, the Montana Lottery, Blue Cross, Providence Health (80,000 employees in five states), large regional banks, Idaho Power, Harrah's, and the UN.

I also had other life plans. By that time my wife and I had lived in Oregon for 14 years and my kids had gone off to college, I had money in the bank, was building a solid nomad-based advertising agency consultation business and had multiple countries on my must-travel-to list.

My business partner and I sold Citrus to another Portland advertising agency. This was a local deal that made sense on many levels.

Reasons to Sell

Owners have a variety of reasons they want to sell their advertising agency. Selling is both a business and personal decision. It's important that the seller really knows why they want to sell and how to get it done at the right price and when.

Here are some key reasons for wanting to sell:

- General industry reasons. The marketing communications industry is always in a state of flux: recession fears, hybrid work systems, new media solutions. You just might be tired of managing constant transformation.
- Agency business reasons. My favorite reason to sell: You are undeniably *unignorable*. So well-known at being an expert that it's time to cash in. I need to stress the expert part. Experts sell faster and at a higher valuation.
- A dream reason. Someone has made you a offer you can't refuse.
- A merger. You're thinking strategically. You want your smaller agency to hook up with a larger agency to help grow the business and to provide major-league experienced guidance. Also, maybe you can offload some of that management time.

Here is a merge-versus-buy quote from Sir Martin Sorrell of S4 Capital that ran in *Media Post*. Remember, that Sorrell built WPP on the back of M&A in the network growth days.

> "Part of Sorrell's disruption strategy, he said, was to find merger candidates as opposed to acquisition candidates. 'If you want to sell, we're not interested,' he said. 'If you want to buy in' and have a 'missionary zeal' for the business, that's what S4 is looking for. Nothing like some skin in the game to keep someone waking up in the morning 'with their heart in their mouth' and focused on success, he added."

- Tired reasons. You are simply tired after years of running and growing an agency. Especially true for over-50-year-old owners. Plus, you have built undeniable value (I hope).
- One more big reason. You have other things you'd like to do. That was a key reason I sold my agency, plus I did not what to reinvent the agency model—yet again.

These are some of the reasons you might want to sell. Regardless of the key business reason, I suggest that you take a deep breath and really understand *your* motivations. Selling an advertising agency at any time can be (will probably be) a long-term journey—a stressful journey.

Understanding your rationale will help you polish your agency and craft the right deal and will dramatically help you to find and entice the right buyer.

How to Sell High

Start here: Visualize your future buyer and their needs. You do this in your business development work. Do that here. Why not create a buyer persona?

CHAPTER 24

I knew that my buyer was probably another west coast agency that would love to have my client list.

It's time to ask a tough question. Please answer this honestly: "Would you buy your agency?"

If the answer is "Yes, I'd buy me," make sure you dig into your rationale and polish your shiny bits. Plus, you better make sure that you're not being delusional.

Would you buy your agency? Yes? Really? You sure?

Does this sound harsh? Believe me, I've seen agency owners think their agency is perfect and desirable only to hear cricket chirps in the marketplace.

If the answer is "No, I would not buy me" and you still want to sell at some point, then you need to pull out those business and marketing plans and take the time to rebuild your agency with a target buyer and their wants in your sights.

A positive note: As you build a better agency for a future sale, you're also building a better agency for today that will attract more new clients. A total win-win even if you don't sell right away.

To get to a new, more beautiful agency, you may need to make some big adjustments.

1. Business model reinvention. How you made money in 2019 might not work in 2025.
2. Find that compelling new or improved positioning. Be unignorable.
3. Add, adjust, or kill current services.
4. Consider brand extensions. Why not add subspecialties that can be discreetly marketed?
5. Manage your client mix. Do not have a client that accounts for more than 30% of billings. Get rid of low-margin clients.
6. Hike up your pricing. Get past having any vestige of being a low-cost supplier.
7. Cut your costs sooner rather than later. Reduce liabilities and debt.

8. Have a sound accounting system. Polish the P&L, balance sheet, and EBITA.
9. See if you can make long-term deals with current clients to keep them happy.
10. Adjust your processes. Efficiency is God. Remember that you can brand your agency processes. Intellectual equity is a good thing.
11. Market the hell out of your agency. Fame is a good thing. Having a solid business development program is a mega plus.
12. Be good looking. The San Diego agency Basic's high-test website, strong positioning, client base (Patagonia, KFC, Google Store), and leadership branding look really good. FYI, Basic was bought by Debt—a large European digital marketing agency based in Amsterdam.

Big point: Build your sales pipeline. Nothing builds interest and a higher valuation more than being able to say we are in discussions with Ferrari and FritoLay.

The Valuation Game

Show me the money. Why not start with the prize. That said, I'm not going into great financial depth here. I'm not an accountant. Or a business broker, which is a sales option, though I'm not a fan of these folks for an agency sale. Agencies are specialized beings.

Agency valuation techniques should be discussed with an M&A specialist or an accountant. I can help you add lots of value to your agency, but I'm not a financial genius. Know what you're good at. If isn't numbers, get an expert. Earlier rather than later.

Valuation Options
- Asset-based valuation. Because your assets are agency brains, I don't believe this calculation makes much sense. This method calculates a

business's equity value as being the fair market value of a company's assets less the fair market value of its liabilities. If you have IP, remember Basecamp—good!
- The multiple. Some gurus use six times EBIDA as a starting point. OK, this initially sounds good. But in real life, this multiple has ranged all over the place. Experts get higher valuations—an integrated agency in Boise not. You need a number, right? My research suggests that you can sell the "average" agency for a three-times multiple.
- If you can, study industry sales comps. It's difficult to impossible to find out about private sales to use as comps. But you can explore reported sales made to public companies such as WPP, the Interpublic Group, Publicis, Omnicom, and consultancies. You can also explore information and news from Adweek, Ad Age, the Drum, the 4A's, and the Association of National Advertisers.

Good luck.

Define Your Agency's Buyer and Their Mind-Set

Do a pros-and-cons buy-or-sell review. Take both sides of the equation. Be brutally honest.

Run an agency SWOT analysis. Consider having multiple people do this to reduce bias and wishful thinking. I have all my advertising agency consultancy clients complete a SWOT analysis before we build business development plans.

Build out scenario planning. What if we do this? What if that?

Write a creative brief to help you develop your sales pitch. You do this for your clients. You are your own client when in agency-sale mode.

I previsualized the sales process as I wrote my Citrus agency sale creative brief. What would I have to do to make the deal happen? What would the buyer need to hear and see? What objections would I need to overcome? What icing could I create to make the agency taste better?

I based my rational understanding of who my target buyer would be on a detailed assessment of our real value and who it would appeal to. It was a delusion-free zone.

Here are the pros and cons we developed.

10 Citrus Pros:
1. We had a well-crafted regional reputation. Reputation is a good thing. A quote from Bob Hoffman, at that time "The Ad Contrarian," in my book on pitching:

    By the way, the best new business program is a good reputation. Duh!

2. Our name-brand client list was regional and national.
3. No single client accounted for more than 20% of agency billings.
4. We priced our agency services correctly. We did not position ourselves as a low-cost agency.
5. We had an active business development program and industry-leading thought leadership. For example, we launched an agency podcast in 2006 (yes, 2006) and ran the blog Recession Freakout in the 2007–2009 downturn. We were forward thinking.
6. We had transferable creative and strategic prowess. The agency that bought us was not as creative.
7. We had a strong balance sheet and P&L. We had a brilliant CFO.
8. We did not have any deal-breaking liabilities or long-term office leases in Bend or Portland.
9. Importantly, I was not critical to the sale. I had been placing myself in the position of not being essential to the management of any account during the preceding two years. I would be an ego-free element of any deal.
10. A plus: The buyer could subtract my salary, bonus and BMW lease from our costs to immediately increase profits.

CHAPTER 24

4 Citrus Cons

There weren't many, as I had been crafting the agency for a sale for over a year.

1. One serious limiting factor was that we were not really an expert agency. We were just an excellent integrated marketing agency. This reduced the pool of potential buyers. Dentsu didn't want a 30-person full-service outpost in Oregon.
2. Portland was already stuffed with creative and savvy tech agencies.
3. A potential con and a plus: I wanted the staff to move to the new agency with their accounts. This was important to me. It was a tough objective, but we met it.
4. Our clients could have revolted and split when they found out about the sale. They didn't because we managed the process and kept key people in place. The deal was managed so the clients understood that all their strategic, creative, and account management benefits remained solid. I wanted the clients to go along with the deal. They did. This was another key reason the buyer needed to keep my staff onboard.

Was I a con in any way? Nope, no con. I wasn't moving with the business and would not be missed. At that point, who cared? But as part of the deal, I was required to stick around for three months.

While sitting and not doing much, I decided that the acquiring agency needed a new, robust business development plan. I accidentally discovered my consultation business. It was to be one of dozens of advertising, digital, design, PR agency plans I have written since I sold.

A Seller Option: Employee Stock Ownership Plan

Consider selling to your employees via an employee stock ownership plan (ESOP). An ESOP is essentially a qualified retirement plan that invests in the company.

I considered an ESOP a few times during my tenure. However, it just looked a bit too complicated for me, and a few casual conversations with employees didn't make me feel optimistic that the type of a deal was right for them.

But exploring an ESOP has its advantages. Here's a list from John Brown's *Forbes* article "Sell to an ESOP: The Most Undervalued Exit Path":

> You may attain financial security through a partial or complete sale of your ownership interest and can stay in effective control until you are paid in full.
>
> A sale to an ESOP can be designed to accommodate your desired departure date whether that date is in a year or several years in the future.
>
> You can leave your businesses gradually.
>
> Owners can remain as president or CEO even after selling all ownership to the ESOP Trust.
>
> There are several tax advantages to the ESOP exit path.

If you have the time to think this through, which means you're not trying to run out your front door tomorrow, you might want to explore an ESOP option with your accountant or exit planner.

Would the idea of selling to my employees have made me feel good? Yes. Did I think I could pull it off? No.

The Earnout Option

Are you willing to take an earnout? To be clear, here is a definition of an earnout from *Investopedia*:

> An earnout is a contractual provision stating that the seller of a business is to obtain additional compensation in the future if the business achieves certain financial goals, which are usually

stated as a percentage of gross sales or earnings.

Earnout or no earnout is an important decision an owner needs to make.

A standard example is some cash up front and quarterly payments based on an adjusted gross income calculation. Most deals go in this direction—it's a contingency plan for the buyer.

FYI: This is what I did in the Citrus sale. I took some cash up front and a three-year earnout based on the adjusted gross income of the accounts we included in the sale. It worked.

Remember, I had set the buying agency up for success: the right crew, solid accounts, strong profit margins, good reputation, and a positive status quo. That said, the new agency lost some of our business in the third year. But the bottom-line was that I was happy by then, still got some quarterly income, and had moved on.

By the time some of the adjusted gross income was declining, I had a profitable advertising agency consulting business and had built a house in the best small city in Mexico and traveled a few months every year since I had became an early digital nomad. My plan worked.

Manage Your Timing

Advertising, digital, PR, and so forth agency sales take time—often a long time. A sale can easily take six months–plus if you talk with multiple dance partners. And all too often a promising deal falls apart during those months of talking.

Here's what I would do in respect to timing:

1. Build out your sales plan. This is your agency's internal plan to create value and a sales scenario.
2. Create an agency "For Sale" calendar to get the job done. This includes all milestones from the initial decision to sell, to designing and marketing the deal you want, to the closing.
3. Hone your business development plan. Look like and act like a

winner. Grow your sales pipeline.
4. Build out enhanced branding to make you look sharp.
5. Create new and improved assets. Got IP? Build it. License it.
6. Dial up branding for you and your key players.
7. Add in the time for lawyers, accountants, M&A guidance, and document creation.

Assume that this sales process from the day you say, "Go—let's find a buyer" to a closed deal can easily take months. In many cases, your patience will deliver more moolah.

Negotiation Or Not

Every sale requires negotiation skills and planning, but *negotiation* is a word that too often strikes fear into agency executives. Agency execs and owners are not good negotiators—they have little to no negotiation training and limited experience.

Don't take my word for it. My *The Levitan Pitch* book includes an interview with Gerry Preece, a 22-year P&G agency services procurement veteran and consultant with Roth Ryan Hayes, a leader in the field of agency search. An unfortunate quote to internalize:

> In 95% of the cases, agencies are babes being led to slaughter. Terrible. Naive. Wishful. They get creamed. They are up against professional negotiators, and they often put their unskilled (in negotiations), nicest, most accommodating people against Procurement. It's generally a blood bath.

Hearing that 95% of P&G agencies are like "babes being led to slaughter" is a painful point to digest. Note that in P&G's case, we're talking about some serious big-time network agencies that don't know how to negotiate.

It's baffling to me that I never took a course in negotiation. Why I didn't try to learn how to negotiate is crazy given the agency industry's need to wrestle every percentage point of margin out of our deals. The only thing that makes me feel better about this deficiency is that I'm clearly not alone.

When To Tell Your Clients

Clients don't like change. Frankly, most will view an agency sale, or merger, as good for the agency and its owners but will question whether it's good for them.

It's therefore critical to know how and when you're going to tell your clients you're selling the agency. There's a balancing act here: You can't spring it on them at the last minute, but you can't bring them on board too early.

My rule: Wait until your sale negotiations are finalized. Just imagine the worst case: You tell the client that you're selling and then the deal falls through. This would not make you look like a genius and could make that client a bit skittish.

Notify your key clients first. Communicate specifics that relate to individual clients, as not all clients will react the same way. Be prepared with answers to the following questions:

1. Who is the new owner? Know what they bring to the party.
2. What is the structure of the new agency? How will it affect the client's account? Could balls be dropped in the transition?
3. What benefits will accrue to the client from the sale? To keep the client happy about the sale, make sure you can tell them why the sale would be good and, importantly, friction-free for them. Put yourself in the client's mindset.
4. What changes to staff and service, if any, might the client experience due to the sale?
5. How involved will the selling agency's management be going forward?

When I told Nike we were selling Citrus, I could tell them that their agency account and creative and production teams would all be moving to the new agency. Furthermore, I could assure Nike that the larger combined agency would provide better service and even fresher thinking. Our big boy Nike said, "Sure thing. Why not?"

Again, every sale and client will be different. But don't tell any client about the sale before you must and before you get your positive good-vibe ducks in a row.

CHAPTER 25

CHAPTER 25

Only One Interview

Going Into Orbit

My book *The Levitan Pitch* includes multiple interviews with industry leaders including the all-important agency search consultant universe*. I decided that this book needs only one interview.

*Yes, I continue to pitch that book.

I recently read Andy Crestodina's book *Content Chemistry: The Illustrated Handbook for Content Marketing*. It's a mind-blowing, very detailed, fully illustrated overview of the world of content marketing. Buy it.

Andy is the cofounder and chief marketing officer of Chicago's 50-person Orbit Media Studios, an expert website development agency.

I gave Andy a shout and we discussed the following, which, not surprisingly, reinforces some of the points I make in this book. In this case, unbelievably brilliant minds think alike.

CHAPTER 25

The interview has been edited for clarity and brevity.

PL: There are so many advertising, digital, and content development agencies. How do you use your book to stand out?

Andy: A way to differentiate is by being the most helpful, informative, generous brand. When I started publishing blog posts 15 years ago, I quickly figured out that the lifespan of a blog post is short, that the value you're putting out in the world is not very durable, and that I could get greater value from this work I was putting in if I was more strategic about it and applied more forethought.

So early on, I put out this hypothesis: If you think ahead and write an outline of everything you know on a topic and then blog into those topics, write articles about each of those subtopics, then you will end up with having not just a list of topics and a bunch of articles, but you'll have a table of contents and a half-written book.

It's partly differentiation. It's partly a sales tool because we send it to prospects, and it makes us look and feel different. So strategically, it's a good strategy because it's efficient, and it solves a problem, and it supports the bottom of the funnel. It supports sales. That's basically it.

PL: I agree that books create differentiation. What other advantages do you get from the printed word?

Andy: In the digital world there's a Back button in front of the reader. A book delivers more of a captive audience. If you can hook them and get them into a printed book, they're reserving more of their time and attention for you than in other formats. There are no notifications, there's no distractions. This book doesn't do anything else. And the fact that it's so visual means that we stopped making an electronic version of it. It's print only. So, I'm really looking for that quality time with the reader, for the chance at better attention and intimacy.

PL: How does the book work into your overall marketing program?

Andy: The book supports sales goals. And prospects are the ultimate target audience. They're the most important target audience. But it also supports marketing goals. It leads to lots of speaking engagements, it leads to conversations like this one, it leads to interviews on podcasts, and it creates a lot of exposure. Books are a differentiated format. Anyone can write a blog post, hit publish, and it goes live. But there's only a smaller percentage of those of us that are willing to take the time, like you're doing, invest all of that research and writing into something bigger.

PL: How do you promote the book?

Andy: The book is sent directly to prospects after meetings. So that's the number one way it gets promoted. The book also is promoted on our website and has been a popular textbook at universities.

The book is in my introduction when I give presentations. We do at least one or two webinars a week. This morning I was interviewed for a podcast. I was asked, "How can people find you?" I say orbit media.com, and I've put all my best into one book called Content Chemistry. You can find it anywhere. It ends up in my introductions, in my interviews, amplified through all of my normal activity.

So, what you just heard was, there's not a specific marketing strategy to promote the book, but we get more value out of all of our visibility because the book is included in everything we do.

PL: What are your thoughts about being a guest on other people's shows—podcasts, for example—versus doing your own?

Andy: Anybody can have a podcast. I've done that as a data-driven marketer. It's a black hole. There's so little data and feedback you get on

CHAPTER 25

podcasts. There aren't good reports for it. It's just an act of faith. Even if you're very, very efficient with the production, it's frustrating to know what it's doing for you.

You rely on anecdotes. Oh, I heard you on that thing. So, my podcast strategy is to be part of other people's shows.

My blog post strategy is very similar. Early-stage content marketers, two-thirds of their content should be on other people's websites. Write for everybody. Write all over the place. I will never stop guest blogging. It's been part of my strategy for 10 years.

PL: Thanks. I'm currently stealing lots of ideas from the book.

CHAPTER 26

A Special Gift for You: Two Instructive Stories

Here's a real-life pitch lesson from my days at Saatchi & Saatchi London. It's a painful story that I hope will help guide you to win more new account pitches. This story is the most read chapter in my *The Levitan Pitch. Buy This Book. Win More Pitches.*

The Worst Advertising Agency Presentation — Ever

I won my first pitch in 1984. I was an account executive at Dancer Fitzgerald Sample, which at the time was New York's largest *Mad Men*-era advertising agency (Saatchi & Saatchi bought DFS in 1987). The pitch was for Western Union's $15 million EasyLink Service. EasyLink was the first commercial email service and launched the same year as the IBM PC—the times were changing fast. We won the pitch, and I learned how a well-oiled pitch worked from a new business team that won nine out of ten pitches that year.

After I began working on the business, I asked Western Union's senior client why we won. She stated three reasons:

1. We took the time to do the research to understand this brand-new market. We arrived with the insight we needed to lead with the benefit of what we called instant mail and not the geeky packet-switching story of electronic mail.
2. She was dazzled by our pitch presentation technology. We used a large bank of slide projectors (this was 1984) to deliver our presentation across a huge screen. Remember, the client was a technologist, and our presentation tools were perfectly mated to her background.
3. She liked us. The people factor matters.

After that first pitch, my batting average was a sweet 1,000.

Not all of my pitches went that smoothly, and over the years I've learned from my winners *and* losers.

Here's the story about the worst, most painful and potentially career-ending advertising agency pitch I've ever been involved in. Let me warn you that it is a sad—but *instructive*—story. You'll learn about hopes and dreams, pitch management, ego management, client psychology, and baby seals.

Saatchi & Saatchi and Adidas

In 1992 Saatchi & Saatchi moved me from New York to London to run business development and the Johnson & Johnson and Sara Lee accounts across Europe and the Middle East. The agency set me up with a sweet expat package that included staff, a nice travel and expenses budget, and a house in Notting Hill. To say this was a cool move and a big job would be an understatement.

Shortly after I arrived, my London friends moved me into what had been Maurice Saatchi's old totally white office before he and Charles headed across town to the more palatial international HQ building. To say that sitting at Maurice's old desk was cool would be yet another understatement.

One day I was in my office with Maurice and Jeremy Sinclair (Saatchi's global executive creative director), and while discussing the agency's new business program, Maurice turned to Jeremy and said, "Boy, we made a lot of bad decisions in *this* office."

As it turned out, I was about to witness them making more bad decisions.

A few weeks after that meeting, Maurice told me we were going to pitch the global Adidas account. Huge brand, global business, cool category, big budget, powerful competition, and a potentially great creative platform. Everything an agency could wish for.

At that time, Nike was on its world domination streak, and Adidas had to step up its marketing. Nike wanted to kick Adidas's butt by taking market share from Adidas's global football business. Adidas was getting nervous. And there's nothing like pitching a highly motivated client that knows it has to step up its marketing.

But wait, wait—there's more... and it was personal. If we won the account, I would open and manage my very own sports marketing agency to run the Adidas account because Saatchi had an existing sporting goods client conflict in the network.

A couple of days later, Maurice and the reclusive Charles Saatchi and I met with Robert Louis Dreyfus, Adidas's new CEO and majority owner, to discuss the pitch. Get this: Robert was a close friend of the agency. He had been the CEO of Saatchi & Saatchi Advertising Worldwide. He was one of us.

One more good thing: Robert asked me to fly from London to Portland, Oregon, to meet with Rob Strasser and Peter Moore, who just started running Adidas America. Rob and Peter were sports industry superstars who helped Phil Knight build Nike and were instrumental in the signing of Michael Jordan. Rob and Peter told me that they wanted

Saatchi to help lead Adidas marketing into the '90s. Adidas needed some Saatchi stardust.

Let's stop for a second and parse this out.

I am working with Maurice and Charles Saatchi—the most famous advertising men in the world.

They asked me to run a huge pitch for the global Adidas account. Adidas's CEO is a close friend of the agency, and the management of Adidas America wants us.

If we won the business, I'd build and run my very own Saatchi sports agency. I was already beginning to visualize a reception area adorned with signed World Cup balls. OK, I was getting ahead of myself.

But wait, there's even more good news: During an early meeting, Robert leans over to me and says, "Peter, you've won this business as long as you don't fuck up the pitch."

I was thinking, the world's best agency doesn't fuck up. I don't fuck up.

The Pitch

I am now about to tell you how we did, in fact, fuck up, and more importantly for you, what I learned.

I think it's important to point out that this was my first big pitch as Saatchi & Saatchi London's business development director. I'm happy to say that I've gotten much better at pitching.

Because Adidas would be such a huge win for the agency, the Saatchi brothers wanted to participate directly in the pitch. A rarity at that stage of their careers.

Because Adidas had so much potential, they wanted me to use the creative talents of Jeremy Sinclair (the agency's global ECD) and Paul Arden, another London creative all-star.

I was now working with Charles, Jeremy, and Paul—three of London's most famous creatives.

Looking good right?

Nope... we started to make a whole set of brand-new mistakes right there in Maurice's old office.

Stay with me, there's a lot of learning here.

Mistake 1

While we all said it was my pitch to run, I had a room full of owners and enormous creative egos (English creative egos are huge) that were difficult to control and were rather opinionated.

Lesson

Every pitch needs to establish one leader and manager. Period.

Mistake 2

My mega-ego creative team was the wrong team for Adidas. They didn't know sports; they didn't want to study the market. And these middle-aged guys did not understand the motivations of the younger sports-shoe consumer. Especially how Nike was killing it.

Paul even called Nike "Nīk." However, despite his mispronunciation, he did have a big idea that was in fact very big.

The idea was that sport is akin to *God*. Sport is a key ingredient in our humanity: It brings out the best in us and it brings the world together. Think of the 2022 Argentina vs. France World Cup game. Through this big idea, Adidas would own the power and humanity of sports itself.

Yes, that's a big idea. Unfortunately...

The Ego Team decided we needed a video for the pitch to deliver the big idea to Adidas. Paul went out on his own, wrote the script, and produced the video. On his own.

To illustrate this big idea, the video included metaphoric images of man's inhumanity to man contrasted with the glory of sports. OK, I got it.

Unfortunately, the imagery went a bit over the top to include individual metaphors like baby seals being beaten on the ice contrasted with the beauty of high jumps. Bloody bloody baby seals!

Cue cringes.

To make matters worse, the video didn't have a budget. You try telling Charles Saatchi how much of his money he could spend on his pitch. The video wound up costing over £30,000.

Lessons

Build the right team for the pitch. In this case the team was primarily based on seniority, not perfect fit. (Note that I also had a savvy account planner and well-oiled pitch team working on the pitch.)

Don't lose control of the process.

Establish a budget going in. Stick with it.

Don't give the creative team too much rope.

By the way, just in case you're thinking I was completely out of my mind, I had asked some of Saatchi London's other award-winning creative teams to come up with alternative ideas that we presented alongside the bloody seals video. Due to the egos of the Ego Team, I had to do this side hustle on the QT.

Mistake 3

I couldn't get these guys to rehearse. I rarely got them in the same room at the same time.

Worse, a couple of days before the pitch, Jeremy began to realize that the baby seal video was going to be difficult to present (a rather large understatement) and told me that I was going to present all the creative work.

Lessons

Assign roles based on expertise not seniority.

Stick to a plan.

Rehearse and rehearse. A lot.

Mistake 4

We knew the CEO Robert Louis Dreyfus well. But we didn't know the

Adidas marketing team. They were not part of the decision to seek a new agency. This pitch was CEO driven.

In fact, we weren't even aware that the Adidas marketing group had already started on a new Adidas campaign approach with London's Leagas Delaney.

Lessons

Know what clients will be in the room and understand their motivations. I should have realized that the Adidas marketing team didn't want to be in the pitch. We could have managed this. But we were so enamored of our relationship with the CEO and access to internal Adidas information that we didn't bother to start relationships with the marketing team before the meeting.

We certainly should have known that beating baby seals to death would alienate virtually everyone in the room. Well, my team knew, but we had lost control of that element of the pitch to the agency's Ego Team by then.

Mistake 5

This is a mistake wrapped up in what's usually a good start. Maurice opened the meeting with a story. Sir Maurice is like the Steve Jobs of agency pitching story telling—with the added benefit of an English accent.

We all know that starting with a relevant attention-getting story is a good thing. However, since we didn't rehearse, we didn't know that Maurice was even going to lead with his story, and we weren't at all prepared to follow along.

The story turned out to be an involved dream sequence about how ancient Egypt, Pharaohs, and Adidas were alike. During the story, even I was spacing out on visions of the Sphinx and pyramids.

In addition to spacing out, I didn't know that Maurice was going to hand the meeting over to me immediately after he talked about my being in his Egyptian dream. I'm sitting there listening to my very own dream, and then I hear, "Take it, Peter."

Lesson

Please rehearse.

Conclusions

Here are all the lessons:
1. Every pitch needs a leader and manager.
2. Never lose control of the process, which should include a timetable and a pitch budget.
3. Make sure that every idea presented is based on an insightful strategy that is developed from a deep understanding of the market and brand. We had done market research, but it didn't directly support the sport as God creative concept.
4. Know which clients will be in the room, their backgrounds, and their motivations. Understanding buyer business and emotional motivations are keys to closing the sale.
5. Assign agency roles based on expertise—not seniority or "hey, it's my turn to pitch." Only your best presenters should ever pitch.
6. Don't give the creative team too much rope.
7. Rehearse.
8. Consider starting with a story. The *right* story.
9. Don't show images of bloodied baby seals.

How Did It all Work Out?

As you might suspect, we did not win the Adidas account, and I didn't get my very own Saatchi & Saatchi sports agency with a reception area wall of World Cup soccer balls.

This pitch, a pitch we should have won, quickly became a famous agency fuck-up story. Fortunately, everyone knew I wasn't solely responsible.

On the positive side, I did learn some powerful lessons and went on to win more pitches in London and New York and have this great story to tell.

Retribution? Yes.

Adidas has never ever been lauded for its advertising. I'm sure that the best creative agency in the world would have helped.

Nike did in fact kick Adidas's global football ass.

We got a good laugh when shortly after the pitch Adidas's marketing team stole Saatchi's brilliant tagline "Nothing is impossible" and humorously reissued it as "Impossible is nothing."

Years after the Adidas debacle my Portland agency Citrus won agency-of-record business from Nike. I finally had my very own sports agency with Nike as a lead client.

A Sad Ad Man "Bye-Bye" Story

This is a personal story about my Nike client. I can't help myself from sharing it.

It is instructive in the sense that it should remind us that the client is the client. They are, at the end of the day, the boss. Not every great idea will get past their boss filter.

How to accept and manage a *no thanks*. Especially when you know that it should be a gleeful yes, is an acquired marketing agency skill better learned early.

A Client's Shortsightedness Helped Me Sell My Advertising Agency

Here's how Nike blew my mind and reinforced my desire to sell my advertising agency. At the time, we were a Nike advertising agency with recurring annual revenues from our Major League Baseball and college sports accounts.

I often talk to agency owners about their plans (hopes, that is) for selling their advertising agency sooner or later. Some are young and are being smart about how to begin to create value for a future sale and some are simply ready to move on – ASAP. Chapter 23 discusses the why and how of selling in detail.

There were many reasons for my heading to the exit. I wanted to move on from running an agency (I had been in advertising and marketing since the 1980's); I was burnt out by the effects of the recession on our profit margin; I didn't want to hear about the next increase in my employee health plan; I did not like watching advertising becoming viewed as a 'commodity'; there were simply too many agencies chasing too few clients; I had some pretty good ideas for creating the "agency of the future" but didn't have the energy to make that happen and, finally, I got way tired of poor client decision-making.

Nike Blew My Mind

One of my agency's' more intelligent B2B clients was Digimarc, a technology firm that essentially *owned* the early QR code market (even the technology behind SoundHound) and, more importantly, digital watermarking, a technology that could turn a graphic or logo into an active QR code. Aim your phone at a QR imprinted logo (a real logo, not a bar code) and it would launch a mobile marketing event. Digimarc called it "The barcode of everything."

One day I brought home a Nike running shoe box and thought that Nike should use the Digimarc technology to activate the Swoosh from being a static graphic to being a very active mobile event launcher. The program was simple, inexpensive and global. Over time, Nike would alert its buyers that there was information and promotional value in aiming their phone at the Swoosh logo. I'm talking millions of boxes that could be brought to life, to tell stories, build the brand and, sell more Nike products.

A SPECIAL GIFT FOR YOU: TWO INSTRUCTIVE STORIES

Just think what Nike could do with the box and related videos: a video message from LeBron, new product intros, deliver promotions, and on and on. I'm like thinking that every one of the millions of currently "DUMB" Nike boxes would all of a sudden become a "SMART" marketing tool.

I asked our direct Nike clients if they'd make an introduction to the senior marketing team to show them how easily and inexpensively (I stress easy and low cost) they could invent a whole new way to add significant value to their packaging. Note, Nike sells hundreds of millions of shoes a year that come in boxes that go directly into people's homes.

I'm thinking… A No-Brainer Idea. Right?

We had the meeting, showed the from dumb box to smart box presentation and instead of pats on our agency backs… we got blank stares. Blank stares! I'm sitting there thinking that this is a major high value / low-cost no-brainer and these guys did not get it. Did not get that for virtually no cost, they could turn their packaging into a significant brand-owned mobile media event. A media and marketing tool that was perfectly targeted to excite Nike's core market which are, of course, major mobile users.

Frankly, this was close to my last agency-life-straw.

It broke my resolve.

I'll try to be kind here. I guess the Nike marketers were busy. But I did have a sense that I was delivering pearls before swine. Am I being harsh? Maybe. That said, I couldn't believe that one of the smartest marketing organizations in the world preferred to send DUMB vs. SMART packaging into millions of homes.

An Update

Look, we have all proposed ideas that clients have not bought. Even brilliant no-brainers. Nike's not buying this idea was shameful.

CHAPTER 26

Years later, the Nike AE that I made the pitch with on that fateful afternoon now works directly for the Nike exec that didn't buy the idea. The exec still remembers my look of total disbelief when they said no thanks.

Of course, today, given the universal use of QR codes, I'd like to think of how far Nike would have been ahead of this graphical mobile marketing curve.

CHAPTER 27

Resources

Four Resources for You

1. Best Advertising Creative Brief
2. Advertising Agency Positioning Statements
3. The Go-No-Go Pitch Quiz
4. Sample Business Development Director Agreement

The Best Advertising Agency Creative Brief

I was trained to use Creative Briefs to build out advertising programs. I've used them for creative work, business development programs and content plans. I used a Creative Brief to help sell my agency. A smart Creative Brief outlines a program's strategic objectives; the target audience and their current thinking; reviews the deliverables; success metrics and the tone of the work. It focuses the mind. Occasionally, I added the question of how the work could be unignorable.

To provide some guidance, I offer an imaginary Creative Brief for a podcast program from the Giant Gorilla agency aimed at the hospitality market. This Creative Brief is designed to make the agency a category thought leader.

A Sample Podcast Creative Brief

CREATIVE BRIEF:
Giant Gorilla Agency Product/Service:
The Marketing Journey Podcast
January _1_202?

Background
London's Giant Gorilla agency specializes in hospitality industry marketing.

It has been successful in building a large client base across a range of industry subcategories. Giant Gorilla is known for its strategic approach, data expertise, high ROI programs, and for its business insights and social media channels.

It is time to move this energy into podcasting.

What is the objective of the project?
Create and produce a daily, brief, unignorable podcast for the hospitality industry. Use the podcast to drive agency awareness and lead gen.

Each show will run for 5 minutes and will includes a brief agency promotion. An example of this style of podcast is The Marketing School podcast from Neil Patel and Eric Siu, it is an example of a quick-take daily listen.

RESOURCES

Who are we talking to?
Listenership will include marketing leadership and press in the food and beverage, lodging and recreation industries.

What do they currently think?
The hospitality industry took a major hit in 2020. Current trends point to growing domestic and international travel. The cash cow of business travel is not expected to reach the highs of 2019 any time soon.

The industry is ripe for the consumption of marketing information related to category growth.

What do we want them to think and what action do we want them to take?
We want the industry to view Giant Gorilla as the leading advertising and marketing communications agency in the hospitality industry. The essence of hospitality has changed, and Giant Gorilla is uniquely positioned to be a leading voice in industry marketing.

What is the message that will move this target audience to action?
Giant Gorilla's The Marketing Journey hospitality podcast delivers business-building information, insights, and brief leadership interviews... every day.

"Give us five minutes every morning and we will help you accelerate your growth."

Program Elements: The Show
The five-minute *The Marketing Journey Show* will be published every weekday at 8 AM EST.

Giant Gorilla's COO Nancy Greene and Creative Director Jill Davis will host The Marketing Journey. Nancy will use her past broadcast experience to lead the discussions. Friendly, intelligent banter will rule.

From time to time, the show will bring in Giant Gorilla's leading thinkers (like CTO Sandy Goddof on TikTok and travel), current clients and guests from the industry.

For production efficiency we will gang record five shows every Tuesday afternoon unless there is late-breaking industry news.

The production team is TBD.

What are the support points?

Timely topics will include news about the business of hospitality: industry trends; what's hot in marketing; the move into new business models; and a range of discussions on the constant evolution of hospitality marketing, with a concentration on digital marketing.

Smart thinking + show personality + great guests = traction & agency brand building.

We have already booked interviews with the CMO of InterContinental Hotels; Shake Shack owner Danny Meyer, a very successful Airbnb host, and the CTO of Hotels.com.

Shows will be supported on the Giant Gorilla website with show notes and links and across social media channels. Guest will be encouraged to promote their episode.

Shows will be used in agency ABM marketing.

What is the brand's character?

The *Marketing Journey* is super smart, knowledgeable, and curious – all with a touch of humor.

What is mandatory?

Each show will be broadcast on all of the major podcast platforms and will be supported by individual show marketing.

Each show will promote Giant Gorilla's hospitality industry expertise. See The Marketing Journey marketing plan for detailed information.

Agency Positioning Statements

I have been hammering the idea that advertising agencies, large, small, single entity must have a brand positioning that stands out for so long that I had to go to ChatGPT for a third-party definition:

> A brand positioning statement is a brief statement that communicates the unique value and identity of a brand. It is typically a sentence or two that captures the essence of what the brand stands for and what sets it apart from its competitors.

OK agencies. Stand out. Be unignorable. Agencies know this. But most agencies are not standing out.

To demonstrate agency sameness (or to be kinder, variety), I've compiled a list from the world of agency descriptions. Before I show the list, it is important to know (I know you know this, but it is always worth keeping it top of mind) ... the competition for creating differentiation is happening daily whether you are a global, regional, local agency or a single entity. The competition for mind-space is fierce. Just imagine being a client trying to make sense of all these words and statements.

I am not trying to tell y'all not to use one of these. Just make sure that the way you express your positioning is designed to make you stand out. Remember that you will need to condense any of these into that 3 floor elevator pitch.

We Are Creative

1. Our work breaks through clutter
2. We are storytellers
3. We design and grow brands
4. We *really* are creative – we mean it! Ask to see our Clios, Lions, D&AD's, Webby Awards and Agency of the Year accolades

CHAPTER 27

We Are Strategic

1. We eat disruption for breakfast
2. We create innovative brand strategies
3. We are a marketing R&D lab with a special sauce
4. We understand the future
5. Our strategy director rocks
6. We deliver and manage customer relationships
7. Our media research drives effective and efficient buys

We've Got Attitude

1. We are nice people
2. We disrupt
3. We are way cool
4. We are ambitious
5. We are client collaborators
6. We are big agency people who built a smaller, more nimble alternative
7. We are nimble
8. We are funny
9. Our agency vision and culture statements are right on
10. We are not dirt bags

We Are Experts

1. We know *your* industry
2. We take challenger brands to #1
3. We've decoded digital advertising
4. We concentrate on B-to-B advertising
5. We are programmatic media experts
6. We get video marketing
7. We are retail + shopper + CRO experts

8. We are demographic experts
9. We create passionate brand relationships
10. Take one of our courses

We Deliver Results

1. We make brands unignorable
2. We crunch big data for breakfast
3. We are all about conversion optimization and ROI
4. Did we say ROI?
5. We deliver engagement
6. We are analytical geniuses

We Deliver Reassurance

1. Our founder wrote, "Whassup?"
2. Our CEO ran marketing at Apple
3. We've designed 157 websites
4. We eat marketing transition for breakfast

We Get Around

1. Think Global
2. Think Global. Act Local.
3. We own your town, state, or region

And you? How do you talk about you?

Wait a minute. So, Peter, how have your agencies positioned themselves?

Dancer Fitzgerald Sample, my 1,000-person NYC Mad Men agency used the line; "*Ambitious Advertising.*" This defined our power-built advertising campaigns and goal of landing the clients that were ambitious. Defining the clients you want isn't a bad approach. Our clients included Toyota, P&G, General Mills, Nabisco and HP.

Saatchi & Saatchi Advertising Worldwide was all about our size (the world's largest) and very British attitude. We used the statement "*Nothing is Impossible.*" It got us British Airways, Gillette, and Schweppes.

My Pacific Northwest agency Citrus told clients that we created advertising that "*Moved consumers to action.*" *Move* was our key deliverable. Our favorite clients were Nike, Dr Martens, Harrah's, and the Montana Lottery.

The Go-No-Go Pitch Quiz

I've pitched for new business from Fortune 100 companies to start-ups to individuals. In all cases, the pitching, i.e., the act of selling and closing a deal isn't easy. It takes work, time, moolah, and will most likely reduce your concentration on the needs of existing clients. Having a plan and a system to decide who to pitch and, as important, not to pitch is a good thing. A very good thing. Here is an approach that can be modified for any type of large or small agency.

You've been asked to respond to an RFP or, potentially better (keyword = potentially), be a finalist in a new business pitch. Great. Now, should you go for it? Should you spend your agency's precious time, staff resources and cash? This is your last chance to make this critical decision.

Since there are so many moving parts to making the all-important 'Go' decision, I developed a quick handy-dandy quiz that you and your senior team can take to help you to decide if you really want to spend the time and money to pitch this account. The quiz will even start to help you think through what you will need to say and do to win the business.

The quiz isolates a set of decision-making criteria and employs easy math to calculate your interest in actually pitching the account. You can, of course, add or subtract criteria. The point is to use some gray matter and time to make the right call.

You do not have to pitch every account that comes knocking. In fact, don't.

A note about your people: Since this is a strategic decision, and you really don't want to show your staff that you are taking a quiz to make the decision, I wouldn't put this in front of the agency or the pitch team. It's just for management. OK, maybe you could share it after the fact to show that you do think through the Go decision-making process.

Each question has three answers ranked from 0 to 3. There is also a bonus question related to incumbency. If your total score is over 10 then you have no choice but to go for it. A 4 to 9 score is where you will have to use your gut and personal experience to make the decision. 3 or less and I'd think hard about ditching the pitch and instead take everyone in the agency out for a beer.

Note: All client, pitch and agency motivations are different. You might want to modify this list depending on your own situation.

The Quiz

1. Do you know the decision maker?
0 – You've never talked to them.
1 – The client came to you through a personal referral.
2 – You are on a first name basis with the client. Maybe you've worked together in the past.

2. Do you have any history with the company?
0 – Never crossed paths.
1 – You worked with someone at the client who can vouch for the quality of your agency.
2 – You worked directly with the client or one of their brands in the past.

CHAPTER 27

3. **How professional is the client's agency selection process? Answer either the client or the agency search consultant questions only. (A or B, not both.)**

    A. Is the person running the pitch experienced?
    0 - They have never ever run a pitch before.
    1 – They are acting professionally.
    2 – They have run pitches before and even sound like they are using the 4A's and ANA pitch guidelines.

    B. Is the client is using a search consultant?
    0 – You don't know the consultant.
    1 – You have pitched the consultant in the past but lost.
    2 – You have won business from the consultant.

4. **Is the client in a category that your agency has targeted?**
    0 – No.
    1 – Yes.
    2 – Yes, and we have a dedicated business development effort to add clients in this specific category.

5. **Do you have direct category experience?**
    0 – You have none. Um, what's a Widget?
    1 – You have worked with a similar company or brand in the client's category.
    2 – You are perceived as being a leading expert in the category. This is probably due to prior client experience and recognized thought leadership.

6. **Do you know the client's budget and / or how they plan to compensate the agency?**
    0 – You have no clue, and the client isn't forthcoming.
    1 – The budget seems low, but you are willing to gamble.

2 – We're in the money!

7. Is the client looking for a "hot" award winning creative agency?
0 – You are creative but are not known for this.
1 – Recent campaigns have gotten you some industry attention.
2 – You have shelves full of Clios and were recently named to the Adweek Agency of the Year Something list.

8. Do you pitch well?
0 – Pitching hasn't been an agency strength.
1 – You have won a third of your pitches.
2 – You are so good at pitching that you have to pinch yourself.

9. How strong is your agency competition?
0 – They really kick ass, have a very high pitch batting average, and you should be worried.
1 – They are very similar to you.
2 – They look weak.

Ladies and gentlemen, your score is _____.

As a reminder: If your score is over 10 then you have no choice but to go for it. 4 to 9 is where you will have to use your gut to make the decision. Less than 3? It's Miller Time down at your local.

A Bonus Question: Are you the incumbent?
Just to complicate matters, are you the incumbent agency? If so, you need to think through why your beloved client has put the account up for grabs. Here is my simple litmus test.

1. You have no clue why the client has put the account up for review.
   Um, without knowing why I'd back way off. It has been reported that only 10% of incumbents keep their account.
2. You are the incumbent, and this is one of those pre-scheduled

procurement-driven reviews. You know that the client loves you. I'd go for it.

If the client has passed your Go-No-Go Quiz then it's time to get to work. Good luck!

Sample Business Development Director Agreement

I am including this sample business development employment agreement as a guide to how to compensate and motivate an agency business development director. Given the high failure rate of this position, we all could use any guidance we can get.

I arrived at this agreement having been a mega agency biz dev director in London and New York; played a key sales role in my Internet-based companies, where a veteran newspaper sales director clued me into how to build an effective comp program and biz dev management experience at my own agency.

The Agreement

Re: Employment with ABC Agency, Inc.

Dear Meagan,

This letter is our formal offer of employment to you and confirms the terms of your employment with Agency, with a starting date of XXX. Should you accept this offer you will serve as a full-time employee in the position of Director of Business Development. Your responsibilities will include, but not be limited to, developing new clients for the agency according to pre-defined client criteria, gathering information about prospects that fit client criteria and preparing research reports to be used in attracting prospects to the agency. In addition, you will make outbound sales calls, appointments for agency meetings and stay in touch with prospects via regular correspondence and mailings.

You will play a key role in managing the agency's response to proposal requests, participating in presentations and if business is successfully won, assure a smooth transition through introduction of the account team for them to take over of the new account. Please refer to the accompanying job description for a more complete review of the responsibilities.

You will receive a monthly salary of $X,000, beginning on your first day on the job, payable on the 15th and last day of each month. You understand that this position carries an exempt status and therefore you will not receive overtime compensation for services performed under this employment arrangement.

In addition to receiving a monthly salary, you will be eligible to increase your income through commissions earned based on obtaining new business for Agency. The program will work as follows:

You must be instrumental in the pursuit and attainment of new clients for Agency based on prospect lists developed with Agency senior management and approved by Agency shareholders. If you are successful in obtaining a meeting with an approved prospect, you will receive a meeting bonus in the pay period following the meeting. Meeting bonus will be $500 less taxes.

If Agency is successful in retaining the client, you will receive a commission based on the client's cumulative earnings. The commission rate will be 5% of AGI (Adjusted Gross Income defined as gross billings collected less direct costs related to those billings) generated on each client acquired. The client must be current with payments and be in good standing in order for commission eligibility. The commission will be paid 45 days after the end of the calendar quarter and will continue for the shorter of up to 2 years from date of first billing or until the business affiliation between Agency and you ceases to exist.

Because business development is such a priority at Agency, we want to reward active employees for their assistance in business development. As such, we want to be clear in identifying what "instrumental" versus

CHAPTER 27

"assistance" means in developing new business. Please see the attached Exhibit A, as a part of this offer letter, and which has been made available to certain existing Agency employees with contacts that may be in a position to bring new business to Agency.

At all times your employment with Agency is "at will". "At will" is defined as allowing either you as the employee or Agency as the employer to terminate your employment at any time, for any reason permitted by law, with or without cause and with or without notice.

You will be eligible for health, vision, life, disability and dental insurance the first of the month following your 30-day employment anniversary. With a start date of XXX, 202X, this coverage would be effective XXX, 202X. As an employee your insurance coverage is paid for by Agency. Any dependents you wish to cover under our group policy will be at your expense.

Please review the Employee Handbook accompanying this letter. Company policy requires that you read this handbook and acknowledge your understanding of Agency policies by signing the acknowledgment that accompanies the Handbook. A copy of the acknowledgment also accompanies this letter. Please return this signed acknowledgment to my attention at your earliest convenience.

All designs, logos, copy, production records, estimates and other material, whether written, printed, or drawn, whether or not subject to copyrighting, made or devised by you or by you with others, will remain the sole and exclusive property of Agency. Upon termination of your employment with Agency for any reason, you shall immediately return to Agency any and all documents and materials containing confidential and proprietary information.

Should your employment with Agency terminate for any reason whatsoever, you agree and understand that for a period of one year from the date of termination you will not solicit or influence any clients, or otherwise divert or attempt to divert, directly or indirectly, any client from Agency that Agency did business with at the time of such termination or had solicited or did business with during the twelve-month period ending on the date of termination.

Also, for one year following such termination, you will not attempt to recruit or hire, directly or indirectly, whether it be as an employee, consultant, agent or representative, on a part-time or full-time basis, anyone who is an employee or independent contractor of Agency now or was an employee or independent contractor of Agency during your association with Agency.

You acknowledge that the restrictions contained in this letter, in view of the nature of the activities in which Agency is engaged, are reasonable and necessary in order to protect the legitimate interests of Agency and that, in addition to all other remedies available to Agency, the Company shall be entitled to injunctive or other appropriate relief. You further acknowledge that Agency has introduced you to its sources of referral, its customer lists, its processes, databases, fee schedules, etc.

If the provisions in the foregoing two paragraphs are found to be overly broad or restrictive, then they will be construed in the broadest manner consistent with applicable law.

If you are in agreement with this offer, please sign and date two copies of this letter where indicated below. As this is being sent via email, return both copies for final signature by Agency, upon which we will return a fully executed copy to you.

We look forward to having you rejoin us as an Agency employee and to a mutually beneficial association.

Very truly yours,
Peter Levitan, CEO

THE AUTHOR

The Author

I like stealing smart ideas. I stole this author format from Derek Sievers who was the mastermind behind CD Baby. I discussed the value of idea theft earlier in the book. If you are going to steal ideas from someone, Derek is a good start. Look him up.

Me In Twenty-Four Seconds

I've been a commercial photographer; an agency owner; an EVP, GM and global business development director at the world's largest agency. I founded two successful early-stage Internet companies. Active Buddy, which presaged Siri and AI, was bought by Microsoft.

I run a global consultancy dedicated to helping advertising agencies make more money.

A New York native, I now live in San Miguel de Allende, Mexico.

THE AUTHOR

You can too. Ask me how.

Me In 2 Minutes

My San Francisco based Levitan & Feinstein Photography worked for San Francisco Magazine, Robert Mondavi Winery, Sonus, and Visa.

I joined New York's largest Mad Men agency Dancer Fitzgerald Sample Advertising in 1980. DFS had golden clients that included P&G, Nabisco, General Mills, Hanes, Wrangler, Toyota and HP. One of my clients invented commercial email. True.

The UK's Saatchi & Saatchi bought DFS in 1986 while I was running the Minneapolis office. Going UK, I started to buy English suits. I won multiple Effie Awards for early-stage content marketing. This was content before we called it content. I called it information as a service.

I moved to Saatchi's London office in the 1990s as European Director, business development director, and managed Johnson & Johnson and other accounts across Europe. I bought more English suits.

I discovered early-stage digital marketing when I returned to New York in 1995. After AOL's President Ted Leonsis told to me to "get the fuck out of advertising" (his exact words) l left the agency to invent the online news industry for the third largest newspaper group. The Newspaper Association of America named me its New Media Pioneer.

In 2000, I launched the startup ActiveBuddy and raised $30 million. We led the world of natural language bots. Our SmarterChild bot had over a billion Instant Messenger conversations across AOL, MSFT, and Yahoo. Microsoft bought the technology in 2006.

I moved to Oregon in 2002 and bought the ad agency Citrus. Our clients included Nike College and MLB AOR programs, multiple banks, healthcare accounts including the five-state Providence, hospitality accounts including Harrah's Casinos, the Montana Lottery, and Legalzoom.

I sold Citrus in 2014. I've bought and sold three agencies. I know the art of buying and selling agencies.

THE AUTHOR

I have spoken at the 4A's, the ANA, Newspaper Association of America, Radio Advertising Bureau, international and regional advertising orgs, and recently at marketing universities across India.

My *The Levitan Pitch. Buy This Book. Win More Pitches.* has guided many agencies in how to run business development. It is an example of how book marketing drives personal brand awareness and business.

What I am Doing Today

I counsel and coach advertising, digital, design, and PR agency leaders across the globe on how to build, manage, and sell kick-ass profitable advertising agencies.

I have over 850 blog posts on business development. This is my fifth book.

A CODA

A Coda

I've covered a lot of territory in this book. All said, if you want to build a kick-ass and way happy advertising agency you need to keep that new client pipeline flowing.

To know how to efficiently get to that wonderful place where you get hired, I asked Lisa Colantuono, President, AAR Partners (the industry's leading agency search consultants) about how clients make the final decision to hire an agency. I believe her response works for any type of client and agency from one person to 1,000. Take it Lisa:

PL: "How does a prospective client make that final agency selection?

Lisa: It's a loaded question and of course, there are many variables involved. One point to keep in mind is that the selection is not based solely on the final presentation but rather the entire process and the progression from beginning to end.

A CODA

Another critical factor is "translation" meaning the agency needs to translate their plans into actionable ideas that make sense and helps the client understand the output.

Of course, "chemistry" or as I prefer, "cultural compatibility" is key.

But after two decades of managing reviews, one client wrapped up making that final agency selection into the simple three Cs: confidence, competence, and cheeriness! You can't have confidence without the competence but be sure to show your assuredness and do it with a smile… In the end, people want to work with people they trust and like."

Now, a Big Request

If you enjoyed this book, please leave me a review on Amazon. I will love you forever.

Ciao.

A CODA

Made in the USA
Las Vegas, NV
23 May 2024